CAREY SCOTT

GOD
CALLS
YOU
beautiful

180
DEVOTIONS
AND PRAYERS
TO INSPIRE
YOUR SOUL

BARBOUR
PUBLISHING

Print ISBN 978-1-64352-710-9

Cover Design: Greg Jackson, Thinkpen Design

Published by Barbour Books, an imprint of Barbour Publishing, Inc., 1810 Barbour Drive, Uhrichsville, Ohio 44683, www.barbourbooks.com

Our mission is to inspire the world with the life-changing message of the Bible.

Member of the
Evangelical Christian
Publishers Association

Printed in China.

Introduction

No matter what the world may say, you are beautiful simply because you're handcrafted by God Himself. You are an intentional creation. The Lord took His time to dream you up, and He wasn't in a bad mood when He did. Others may say you're too much or too little. They may say you're too messy or too full of drama. They may not like the way you look, the way you talk, or the way you choose to live your life. But they measure with worldly standards, not godly ones. And the goal of your life isn't perfection. It's living with purpose and passion for the Lord. So don't let the world's labels stick, because the God of all creation calls you beautiful. And He always will.

Beauty from the Inside Out

*Those who give thanks that Jesus is the
Son of God live in God, and God lives in them.*
1 JOHN 4:15 TPT

What a privilege to have God's Holy Spirit living in us. It's a gift we receive for recognizing Jesus as the Son of God and accepting Him as our Savior. It's a deposit of goodness that creates beauty within us—beauty that radiates from the inside out. And if we embrace the powerful transformation the Spirit brings, we will shine Jesus into a world that needs hope.

Breathe that truth in again, friend. God chooses to live in you. While the world may not understand all you have to offer, He certainly does. God knows the unique qualities that make you a force for truth. He sees the hard choices you make to love Him and others well and recognizes the countless sacrifices along the way. To God, your pursuit of righteous living is a beautiful example of holy living. You delight Him even in your missteps and mishaps, and God calls you beautiful regardless of what others may think.

....

*Father, I cherish Your Holy Spirit in me. I realize the beauty of
that gift. And I'm grateful knowing Your presence makes me pleasing
in Your eyes. Help me shine You to the world. Help my life convince
others of their need for You. In Jesus' name I pray. Amen.*

Where True Beauty Comes From

Let your true beauty come from your inner personality, not a focus on the external. For lasting beauty comes from a gentle and peaceful spirit, which is precious in God's sight and is much more important than the outward adornment of elaborate hair, jewelry, and fine clothes.

1 PETER 3:3–4 TPT

What a different perspective than the one we hear from the world. Peter is reminding us of where our true beauty comes from, and it isn't from our appearance. Shocker, right? Every day, we're bombarded with images of photoshopped women who look perfect. We scroll through social media and measure our beauty against what advertisers tell us is acceptable. We compare our frumpy days to our online friend's trendy style and decide we're a hot mess. Stop.

Your true beauty comes from within. A gentle spirit, a kind heart, a peaceful presence. . .these are how God measures your beauty. These are what delight the Lord. A toned tushy, lovely locks, a flawless face—none of these will last. But your inner personality matters far more than those things ever will. And it's by those internal measurements that God calls you beautiful.

....

Father, I'm so glad You see beauty differently than the world, because trying to keep up with their standards is exhausting. Thank You for seeing the real me and loving my imperfect perfection. You're the best. In Jesus' name I pray. Amen.

Fake News

So we have no reason to despair. Despite the fact that our outer humanity is falling apart and decaying, our inner humanity is breathing in new life every day.

2 Corinthians 4:16 voice

How many times have you reached for the fountain of youth? No judgment, friend! If we were all super honest, we'd admit to believing fake news that tells us this potion or pill has the power to beat the effects of aging. We've probably tried a gimmick or diet fad a time or two. And maybe we've bought into a miracle workout craze that made huge promises it never delivered on. In a world that changes and fades with time, why do we think we won't?

Here's where we can believe God's good news instead. While your body may be aging, your inner beauty isn't. Every day, it's renewed in Him. It can remain young, sweet, and spunky regardless of what years are doing to the outside of you. Because your spirit stays alive and spry, there's no reason to dwell on your dwindling human condition. Whether you're flourishing or feel like you're falling apart, God calls you beautiful.

....

Father, how awesome that my inner humanity isn't prey to the effects of time. Help me not to focus on the fake news the world offers that tells me staying young on the outside is the goal. It isn't! I see that now. Thank You! In Jesus' name I pray. Amen.

You Are Poetry!

*We have become his poetry, a re-created people that will fulfill
the destiny he has given each of us, for we are joined to Jesus,
the Anointed One. Even before we were born, God planned in
advance our destiny and the good works we would do to fulfill it!*

EPHESIANS 2:10 TPT

The dictionary defines *poetry* as something marked by a special intensity of expression. It's a quality demonstration of creativity. It's regarded as beauty. It's designed to stir emotions. Poetry is full of powerful feelings. And, sweet one, you are these things to the Lord!

The world may be quick to cast you aside, leaving you feeling worthless. It may not celebrate your God-given unique and beautiful qualities. And it may leave you feeling puny rather than poetic.

But that will never negate that you're His handiwork, a one-of-a-kind piece of art He purposefully planned. Your Creator thought of everything—your talents, appearance, personality, destiny, good works—even your entrance onto the kingdom calendar. He dreamed you up with passion and intentionality. Once done, God beamed with pride, calling His creation good. And because you're His poetry, He delights in your beauty.

....

*Father, I love knowing You took intentional time to create me.
To know the God of all creation thought me up is a powerful reminder
of my value. In those times I feel overlooked and unloved, bring this
truth to mind. It changes everything. In Jesus' name I pray. Amen.*

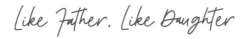

Like Father, Like Daughter

*So God created man in His own image, in the image and
likeness of God He created him; male and female He created them.*
GENESIS 1:27 AMP

Not only were you created by God, but you were also made in His image and likeness. Think about it. Do you think God is trash? Do you think He's not good enough? Do you believe He's lacking or unlovable? Chances are you find God inspiring and worthy of praise and adoration. You may not always understand His will and ways, but you know He is inherently good.

Scripture says we're made in His image and likeness. That means we can choose to have a strong character marked by integrity. We can be wise and discerning. We can have peace, patience, joy, kindness, self-control, goodness, faithfulness, and gentleness. We can be faithful friends and trustworthy confidantes. Because we resemble our Father, we can access heavenly traits to live out here on earth.

A life aligned with God's will is something beautiful to behold. Reflecting Him to the world is an honor and a privilege. And it's this deliberate choice to be like God that makes us lovely in His eyes.

....

*Father, what a joy and privilege to be created in Your image and likeness!
Help me steward this gift well. Give me courage to stand in that truth when
giving in to the world's way would be easier. In Jesus' name I pray. Amen.*

Wither and Fade

The grass withers, the flower fades; nothing lasts
except the word of our God. It will stand forever.
ISAIAH 40:8 VOICE

Let's set realistic expectations for ourselves, ones supported by scripture. If we don't, our hearts will be troubled by what we see. We'll struggle to be content with our dwindling energy and stamina. We'll fall into the trap of comparison, jealous we can't keep up with others like we did before. We will risk being angry because we can't maintain the beauty standards of the world. Unrealistic expectations will keep us in chaos and prevent us from finding joy in the withering and fading—something every one of us will experience.

The truth is that you will age. Your body and mind will decline. You won't be able to do all the things you once did. But that won't take away any value in who you are as a woman, so don't partner with the lie that says it will. Continue this beautiful journey with your family and friends. . .and your heavenly Father. He is the one thing that will never wither or fade. And no matter what the years do to you, He always calls you beautiful.

. . . .

Father, help me find peace in the withering and fading. It's just
part of life and there's nothing I can do to stop it. Help me be content
with my changing body through the years so I can be marked by
contentment in You. In Jesus' name I pray. Amen.

A Beautiful Mind

*So keep your thoughts continually fixed on all that is authentic
and real, honorable and admirable, beautiful and respectful,
pure and holy, merciful and kind. And fasten your thoughts
on every glorious work of God, praising him always.*
PHILIPPIANS 4:8 TPT

What you think about affects what you do. Your thoughts eventually come out in your words and actions. It's impossible to think honorably of someone and treat them with disdain. The reverse is true as well. If you camp on thoughts of hate, anger, jealousy, frustration, or unforgiveness toward another, that's how you'll treat them. Your thoughts run your life, which is why God warns us to focus on things authentic, admirable, beautiful, holy, and kind.

Are you struggling with your thought-life? Do you focus on joy-draining ideas and notions? Are you often thinking negatively about people, replaying offenses and plotting revenge? Would those around you say you're a cup-half-empty kind of woman these days? It's easy to focus on the wrong things, friend. Life is hard. So rather than live there, why not ask the Lord to shift your focus to things that are admirable? It will change how you interact with others, and God will be pleased with your beautiful mind.

*Father, help me keep my thoughts fixed on things that are good and holy.
I know my thoughts affect my actions, and I want to live a beautiful life
as I bless others and glorify You. In Jesus' name I pray. Amen.*

Celebrating Your Mysterious Complexity

I thank you, God, for making me so mysteriously complex!
Everything you do is marvelously breathtaking. It simply amazes
me to think about it! How thoroughly you know me, Lord!

PSALM 139:14 TPT

What if you decided to celebrate everything that made you unique rather than made excuses for those things? What if you embraced your quirky ways and wacky sense of humor? What if you didn't see your messy moments as an inconvenience to others? And what if all the things that make you different—make you, you—were labeled delightful rather than dysfunctional?

Listen, friend, the world is quick to tell us we're weird if we go outside the predetermined boundaries set for us. Think about it. Have you ever received a condemning glance from a stranger, a reprimand for a unique expression of excitement, or a reminder to conform so you'll be acceptable? Don't let these stick! You be you, and let them be them. Your Father in heaven decided to make you special and delights in who you are. And knowing all your glorious and mysterious complexities, God calls you beautiful.

....

Father, it's so hard not to feel self-conscious about who I am and
what I do. Sometimes insecurity keeps me hidden rather than living
out loud. Would You give me confidence and courage to be the
woman You created me to be? I want to celebrate the mysterious
complexity You gave me! In Jesus' name I pray. Amen.

The Secret to a Beautiful Life

A mind focused on the flesh is doomed to death, but a mind focused on the Spirit will find full life and complete peace.
ROMANS 8:6 VOICE

In the verse above, Paul dropped a huge truth bomb. Don't miss it, because it's a power-packed gold nugget for a beautiful life. It's all about what you choose to focus on. Will you spend your one and only life following the world's trends and killing yourself to keep up, or will you instead fix your mind on God's goodness? Will you work yourself to the bone to fit in or decide there is more important kingdom-focused work to be done?

It's easy to get caught up in the things of the day. We get sucked into the details of friend or family drama or drench our minds with useless celebrity gossip. We become unhealthy in working out or dieting or following the latest fashion trends, consuming our time and minds with staying relevant. But when we instead focus on the Lord—serving, praising, worshipping—we will be rewarded with a fulfilling life and complete peace. God promises to bless your obedience to fix your attention on His will and ways, and He will call your choice to focus on Him a beautiful one.

Father, help me focus my mind on You and not my fleshly desires and pleasures. I want a full, beautiful life and complete peace with You. In Jesus' name I pray. Amen.

Every Part of You

Every part of you is so beautiful, my darling.
Perfect is your beauty, without flaw within.
SONG OF SONGS 4:7 TPT

In God's eyes, every part of you is beautiful. He should know. He's the One who created you to His idea of perfection. That means the stretch marks and scars, the places where gravity has taken charge, your thinning hair or patches of acne, the gap in your teeth or wrinkled skin. . .every part is acceptable to your God. This truth is in stark contrast to what the world says.

The world sets forth high expectations of beauty that are never fully attainable or maintainable. The problem is that the more we entertain lies about our beauty and goodness, the easier they are to believe, and we eventually allow them to usurp God's truth. And rather than believe we're beautiful, we instead focus on each and every flaw, robbing ourselves of His peace and falling into the trap of comparison where we never feel good enough.

Choose this day to allow the Lord to have the last word in your heart. Choose to believe Him over anyone else. Decide to see yourself through His eyes. And know that without a doubt, your Father in heaven calls every part of you beautiful.

....

Father, thank You for finding me beautiful. Sometimes it's
hard to accept. Would You please give me the confidence
I need to live in that truth? In Jesus' name I pray. Amen.

Your Banner of Beauty

*Nor should you worry about clothes. Consider the lilies of the field
and how they grow. They do not work or weave or sew, and yet
their garments are stunning. Even King Solomon, dressed in
his most regal garb, was not as lovely as these lilies.*

MATTHEW 6:28–29 VOICE

Sometimes we get it all wrong. We decide beauty is based on our wardrobe, so we make sure our closet is stocked with the latest fashion trends. We think beauty is based on our looks, so we spend our time and treasure coloring our hair, attending CrossFit, getting surgical alterations, pampering ourselves with facials and treatments, and plucking and tucking where we can. But all these things amount to an empty well because the results are fleeting. We're either competing or trying to impress. Either way, this mind-set leaves us striving for the wrong kind of beauty.

God made you exactly the way He intended you to be. He knew gravity would be a factor. He knew you'd be tempted to follow the world's ideals and standards. And He knew one day you'd be reading this very devotional. His message to you today is simple. Friend, even with every wrinkle, bump, lump, and rogue hair, your heavenly Father calls you beautiful. Let that be your banner of beauty.

....

*Father, I hear You. I'm grateful for the timing of this message.
Thank You for seeing me and knowing exactly what I needed
to read today. In Jesus' name I pray. Amen.*

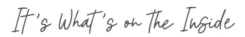

It's What's on the Inside

Women, the same goes for you: dress properly, modestly,
and appropriately. Don't get carried away in grooming your hair
or seek beauty in glittering gold, pearls, or expensive clothes.
Instead, as is fitting, let good works decorate your true beauty and
show that you are a woman who claims reverence for God.

1 TIMOTHY 2:9–10 VOICE

Simply put, true beauty comes from within. The writer of this scripture passage isn't shaming you for caring about what you look like. He isn't telling you to dress in sackcloth with ratty hair and smeared mascara from the day before. Instead, this passage is an encouragement that it's what's on the inside that matters.

Have you known someone who may not be considered beautiful according to the world's standards, but who is so kind and caring that they're beautiful in your eyes? On the flip side, have you known someone who appears to be perfect on the outside but is mean as a snake, self-serving, and downright rude? No amount of makeup and designer clothing can cover up meanspiritedness. Amen?

When you live and love others well, your true beauty can't help but radiate from the inside out. And when it does, God will delight in who He created you to be and will call you beautiful.

....

Father, help me remember worldly beauty is only skin deep,
but true beauty is what matters the most. That's the kind of
beauty I want to be known for. In Jesus' name I pray. Amen.

What Does God Consider?

*Take no notice of his looks or his height. He is not the one,
for the Eternal One does not pay attention to what
humans value. Humans only care about the external
appearance, but the Eternal considers the inner character.*

1 SAMUEL 16:7 VOICE

How would your life be different if you truly believed this verse? Think about how your insecurities would diminish. Think about how your fears of not being good enough would dissipate. Knowing that character is the measurement for beauty rather than the way you look on the outside can build your confidence and give you courage to be yourself. And that's exactly God's hope for you.

The stakes are high. As women, we can become fixated on what the world thinks and ignore what God considers as truth. We can strive to become acceptable in society's eyes—working ourselves to the bone to become worthy of love—and miss the fact that God already and always calls us beautiful. But when we choose to grab onto the truth that our inner character is what matters, we'll live in the freedom of who we were created to be.

. . . .

*Father, I'm so grateful You look at what's on the inside. I struggle
to believe this truth sometimes because it's in opposition to the
world's way of thinking, but I am choosing today to consider
the things You consider. In Jesus' name I pray. Amen.*

Everything Has Beauty

He has made everything beautiful and appropriate in its time. He has also planted eternity [a sense of divine purpose] in the human heart [a mysterious longing which nothing under the sun can satisfy, except God]—yet man cannot find out (comprehend, grasp) what God has done (His overall plan) from the beginning to the end.
ECCLESIASTES 3:11 AMP

Reread the first sentence of the scripture above. Notice it says God made *everything* beautiful. It doesn't say He made some things beautiful. It doesn't say He made everything with the potential to be beautiful. This powerful passage doesn't mince words, nor is it laden with big, confusing words. It simply tells us that *everything* God made has beauty. Grab that truth, friend.

The world most certainly has its opinions and isn't shy to weigh in on the standards it sets for beauty. And while God's Word may tell us that every single thing He made is full of magnificence and splendor, so often—too often—we subscribe to the world's ideals. Today, ask God to renew your mind so you can live in the truth that God calls you beautiful.

Father, why is this so hard to believe? I need Your help to change my mind-set so I can rest knowing that no matter what the world tells me, Your constant reminder is that I am lovely. In Jesus' name I pray. Amen.

Clothed with Christ

For you [who are born-again have been reborn from above—spiritually transformed, renewed, sanctified and] are all children of God [set apart for His purpose with full rights and privileges] through faith in Christ Jesus. For all of you who were baptized into Christ [into a spiritual union with the Christ, the Anointed] have clothed yourselves with Christ [that is, you have taken on His characteristics and values].
GALATIANS 3:26–27 AMP

Can't afford those fancy designer clothes? Don't feel comfortable wearing those kinds of styles? Can't imagine paying hundreds of dollars for threads and soles? Well then, you are in luck, friend! Why? Because when you said yes to Jesus as the Lord and Savior of your life, you were instantly given a new sense of fashion. You were clothed with Christ.

That means you are now wearing His character. You are sporting His kindness and compassion. You're all dolled up in love and mercy. You're dressed in wisdom and discernment. Every day, you are putting on peace and patience. And when God looks at you, His daughter, He calls you beautiful.

....

Father, I've never given much thought to the new sense of style I received when I said yes to Jesus. I love knowing I am clothed in such goodness. Thank You for giving me all I need to live and love well. I'm going to wear these clothes well. In Jesus' name I pray. Amen.

What Keeps You from Believing?

No gem is more precious than she is—your most
extravagant desire doesn't come close to her.
PROVERBS 3:15 VOICE

You are precious to God. The world may beat you up and tell you you're worthless. You may have daily reminders that you're unattractive or unlovable. You may never experience the kind of worldly acceptance you crave. And you may always feel *less* than others around you. But, sweet friend, the One who created you is completely enamored with who He made you to be.

What would need to change for you to see yourself as God does? What keeps you from believing you are treasurable? Do you need to stop negative self-talk or ask someone else to stop being so critical? Do you need to change your friend group and spend more time with those who encourage instead? Maybe you could change what you're reading or watching. Are you focusing on fashion, fitness, or food and it's making you strive for the wrong things? Today, take inventory to help you better understand what's causing your self-doubt. And then thank the Lord that He sees your value and always—no matter what—calls you beautiful!

....

Father, I know I need to make some changes because I am constantly
feeling worthless. It means so much that You continually see my value.
Would You help me get to the root of my struggle with self-acceptance
and overcome it? I love You. In Jesus' name I pray. Amen.

Rooted in the Lord

She is like a tree that produces a satisfied life for
anyone who can wrap their arms around her;
happiness waits for any who hold her tightly.
PROVERBS 3:18 VOICE

Being intentional in your time with God yields in you beautiful gifts you can give to others. You'll be able to bring a sense of peace and a much-needed calm to your family. When you're rooted in your relationship with the Lord, your friends will be blessed by your testimony of faith. Your joy and happiness will produce those in people around you. And your wisdom and godly perspective will help others find contentment in their own lives.

Choose to invest in your faith. Spend time in God's Word. Pray often and about everything. Saturate yourself with praise music and life-giving sermons. Find community with like-minded believers and look for ways to bless others. Be deliberate to grow in your relationship with God, because He is your source—the One who will give you depth to be a blessing to those in your sphere of influence. And because your heart is to be a blessing to others, He calls that gift in you beautiful!

....

Father, I want to be this kind of woman to my friends and family.
Help me bless them by staying rooted in You. I know You are the
reason I can love others well. In Jesus' name I pray. Amen.

Be Humble

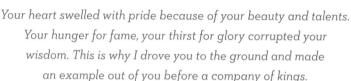

Your heart swelled with pride because of your beauty and talents.
Your hunger for fame, your thirst for glory corrupted your
wisdom. This is why I drove you to the ground and made
an example out of you before a company of kings.
EZEKIEL 28:17 VOICE

This passage of scripture is a red flag warning. Maybe God includes these kinds of accounts so we will know ahead of time the attitudes, beliefs, and actions that can get us into trouble. His warnings are kind, really. Like any good parent, our Father wants to protect us from harm and hurt. And this is one of those reminders that will save us from His tough-love correction.

Be humble. We may have great hair, tanned skin, impressive abs, and piercing eyes, but those things should not define us. We may be smart as a whip, unbelievably creative, super strategic, or able to multitask like no other, but we need a healthy perspective. When we choose to focus on these assets too much, we elevate them. Then we elevate ourselves. And the truth is that pride is an ugly quality. God sees humility as a beautiful quality. Friend, let Him see that in you.

Father, would You help me find the perfect balance between too little and
too much confidence? I want to be able to recognize the gifts You've
given me without falling into the pit of pride. Please give me the right
dose of humility and self-assurance. In Jesus' name I pray. Amen.

A Beautiful Commitment

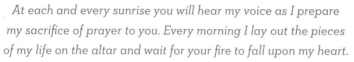

*At each and every sunrise you will hear my voice as I prepare
my sacrifice of prayer to you. Every morning I lay out the pieces
of my life on the altar and wait for your fire to fall upon my heart.*

PSALM 5:3 TPT

The psalmist has made a pledge to invest in his relationship with God. He knows how vital it is to start and end each day with the Lord. He understands the benefit of connecting every part of his life to God. And he sees the value of patience as he waits expectantly for the Lord's answer and direction. That's a beautiful commitment.

God's greatest desire is to have a daily connection with His creation. He craves community with you. He may be all-knowing, but that never trumps His desire to hear your problems and praises from your lips. The Lord is ready to meet with you whenever you need Him. Whether you need wisdom, peace, hope, help, or just a listening ear so you can vent, know that God is waiting to hear from you. And when you—like the psalmist—see the value and benefit of linking your heart to God's, it will change your life. And He will call that kind of commitment from you beautiful.

....

*Father, I want You to be involved in every part
of my day. Thank You for wanting the same
from me. In Jesus' name I pray. Amen.*

The Ugliness of Shame

But in the depths of my heart I truly know that you, Yahweh, have become my Shield; you take me and surround me with yourself. Your glory covers me continually. You lift high my head when I bow low in shame.

PSALM 3:3 TPT

There is no reason to feel shame when you're a believer, but that doesn't mean you won't feel it. Let's be honest: there's no shortage of opportunities to be embarrassed for being too much or too little. It's not hard to find places where we feel less than others. Social media invites jealousy as we compare ourselves with others. And chances are you hear messages daily that tell you you're not good enough.

But Jesus gave His precious life to permanently remove your shame. It's ugly on you because it drains your joy and spark. It tells you that you are broken. That you're not okay. And that's the opposite of who God says you are. Friend, ask the Lord to lift your head and remove the shame you've been carrying. You were created for so much more. Let God give you the confidence to live in the beauty He created you to carry.

....

Father, what a wonderful gift to not have to wear shame any longer. Would You remind me of who I am in You, and give me the courage to choose that truth every day? In Jesus' name I pray. Amen.

The Beautiful Ways of God

The beautiful ways of God are a safe resting place
for those who have integrity. But to those who work
wickedness the ways of God spell doom.

PROVERBS 10:29 TPT

In a world of wickedness and every evil way, God reminds us that honesty and truthfulness open heavenly doors. A gift is waiting on the other side of your integrity. The Lord promises to protect good people. He gives favor to the upright. He promises us peace in chaos and patience in the waiting. He blesses us with wisdom and discernment. Your good choices delight Him so much that He provides safety and rest. He rejoices when you have the gumption to stand up for what's right!

Where is integrity a challenge in your life? Is living authentically and honestly difficult for you? Are you struggling to stay on moral high ground? Remember that your choices come with consequences or blessings. When you decide to honor God in your decisions, He sees your courageousness and is filled with pleasure!

....

Father, it's so easy to fall in line with the world's ways. Please forgive
me for all the times I've walked the easy path of bad choices. I don't
want that anymore. Instead, I want to live differently. I want my life
to be full of integrity, making You proud of my choices to glorify
You and benefit me. I want to experience all the beautiful ways
You bless our lives! In Jesus' name I pray. Amen.

Never Tossed Away

And when you are old, I will still be there, carrying you. When your
limbs grow tired, your eyes are weak, and your hair a silvery gray,
I will carry you as I always have. I will carry you and save you.
ISAIAH 46:4 VOICE

The truth is that we will grow old and our bodies will fail us. It's just part of the human condition we all will face. And while the world may decide we're no longer relevant, God will never feel that way. Others may consider us a burden, but the Lord continues to see our immeasurable worth. Our beauty may not meet worldly standards, our minds may slow, and our bodies may weaken, but He will delight in us as much as ever. In God's eyes, our increasing age never decreases our value.

Wasn't God kind to include this verse in His Word? It's one of those scriptures that calms an anxious heart. It's a promise He wants to settle in your heart today. And it's a beautiful assurance that you will always have value and that God will always take care of you. No matter what, your caring Father will always call you lovely and worthy!

Father, what a relief to know I will never lose significance to You. Thank
You for promising me companionship throughout my life, until I see You
face-to-face. Lord, You really are all I need. In Jesus' name I pray. Amen.

You Are Worth Protecting

His massive arms are wrapped around you, protecting you.
You can run under his covering of majesty and hide. His
arms of faithfulness are a shield keeping you from harm.
PSALM 91:4 TPT

It's natural to want to protect what we care about the most. The urge to safe-guard those we love is a strong, innate reaction. That sense of justice can rise up in defense for our family and friends in an instant. And just as you would do whatever it takes to protect your children, spouse, or friends, the Lord feels that same way about you. He fiercely protects His prized possession.

Where do you need God's massive arms to surround you right now? Where do you feel vulnerable and unprotected? Where do you need reassurance that you are safe and fortified? God wants you to know that you are worth protecting. You are worthy of a safe place with Him. And it's in His arms of faithfulness that you will be shielded from people and situations that threaten. The world may not, but God will always call you worthy.

....

Father, I'm scared. I feel vulnerable and unsafe. I don't know how I got into
this mess, but I am desperate for Your help. Please wrap me up in Your love
and protection. I need Your help to make it through. Thank You for seeing
my value and always being there for me. In Jesus' name I pray. Amen.

Loving the Lord Is Beautiful

*Charm can be deceptive and physical beauty will
not last, but a woman who reveres the Eternal
should be praised above all others.*
PROVERBS 31:30 VOICE

True beauty isn't about what's on the outside. Scripture tells us those things are fleeting. The ability to captivate others with charm and allure will not last forever. Outward beauty has a shelf life, and time and gravity will eventually take their toll no matter how much effort we put toward preserving our youth. Choosing to allow these earthly measurements to determine your value as a woman will always leave you wanting for more. They will never be an accurate gauge of your significance. Be careful you don't let them be.

God is clear that the most praiseworthy trait is to be the kind of woman who loves the Lord. Having respect for Him as we live and love is commendable. And while the world may tell you that womanhood is about perfect skin, a toned body, fashionable clothing, and other outward-focused standards, the Lord reminds us what true beauty is—an intentional relationship with Him. Now, friend, *that* is beautiful.

....

*Father, help me love You. Give me the courage to choose my
relationship with You over anything else the world has to offer.
Remind me that it's in You my womanhood is anchored and not in
any form of worldly charm or beauty. In Jesus' name I pray. Amen.*

Labeled

*Dear friends, My name is Paul, and I was chosen
by God to be an apostle of Jesus, the Messiah.*
EPHESIANS 1:1 TPT

There is something beautiful about knowing who you are. It's easy to allow the world to put all sorts of labels on you, like high-maintenance, prideful, messy, controlling. And honestly, there may be some truth to them. We're not perfect, right? But be careful, because when we adopt these labels as our identity, they affect our confidence. How we act or respond isn't always a good indicator of who we really are.

As he's introducing himself to the church in Ephesus, Paul boldly states his name and his purpose. He confidently knows his true identity and makes no excuses. His self-assurance is noteworthy. And while there's no doubt he was known for being many things—persecutor, hypocrite, Christian, encourager—Paul embraces his label of chosen.

What about you, friend? You get to choose too. Will you adopt the labels the world sticks to you, or will you allow God's labels of lovely, chosen, loved, forgiven, and redeemed to stick instead? Forget who *others* say you are and live with confidence, knowing God calls you beautiful.

....

*Father, it's so hard to feel good about myself knowing I'm not who the world
says I should be. I confess I listen to the world's voices way too often. Help
me choose to believe what You say instead. In Jesus' name I pray. Amen.*

The Beauty of Steadfast Faith

*My children, you have come from God and have
conquered these spirits because the One who lives
within you is greater than the one in this world.*

1 JOHN 4:4 VOICE

Don't be afraid of the evil in the world, sweet one. It's no match for God. Sometimes it's hard to cling to this truth, especially when we immerse ourselves in the dire news delivered to us every minute of every day. It's hard to hold on when we feel hated and oppressed by others. And it's hard to believe evil can't win when we're feeling hopeless. But when we give in to this mind-set, we're forgetting that our God is bigger than anything the world can throw at us. He is greater than it all.

You can choose today to have the kind of steadfast faith that is unshakable in the face of evil. You can kick fear to the curb and give it no space in your head or heart. You can choose radical faith that knows God has everything under control. And when you do, He will call that decision beautiful and bless you for it.

....

*Father, I am choosing to trust You in all things. I will remember that
You are always greater than any heartache or discouragement that
comes my way. I will stand strong and look to You for strength and
peace when I need it. You are awesome! In Jesus' name I pray. Amen*

Meant to Melt Your Heart

*Do the riches of his extraordinary kindness make you take him
for granted and despise him? Haven't you experienced how kind
and understanding he has been to you? Don't mistake his tolerance
for acceptance. Do you realize that all the wealth of his extravagant
kindness is meant to melt your heart and lead you into repentance?*

ROMANS 2:4 TPT

Take a moment to think of all the ways God has been kind to you in the past week. Nothing is coincidence or luck. All good things come from Him. So as you look back on the last seven days, where has God's kindness revealed itself? Maybe the call came, the money showed up, the door opened, the apology was given, or the fear dissipated. It's that kind of extravagant kindness that's meant to thaw out and soften your heart for repentance and restoration.

Watch for God's gentleness and generosity. Be aware of the ways He's trying to get your attention, knowing He has a divine purpose. Always show gratitude for every good thing, never taking for granted His blessings. This kind of intentional living is a beautiful response to a loving God.

....

*Father, give me ears to hear and eyes to see what You are doing
in my life. Help me be grateful rather than greedy. Help me be aware
of Your kindness and appreciative for it. And lead me into repentance
so I can be richer in You! In Jesus' name I pray. Amen.*

Imitate That Which Is Lovely

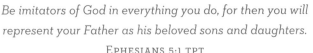

*Be imitators of God in everything you do, for then you will
represent your Father as his beloved sons and daughters.*

EPHESIANS 5:1 TPT

Act like God. Reflect His character to others. Be the kind of woman who loves unconditionally and forgives without fail. Live unoffended, always ready to respond with grace. Show kindness to everyone, no matter what. Be generous with your time and treasure. Treat others with respect and honor. Show self-control in your anger, and make sure not to use words as weapons. Bring peace into chaotic situations. Show patience in the waiting, trusting that the Lord is working all things for your good. Make sure your actions come from pure motivations and point others to your Father in heaven. Surrender control to the Creator. And don't let anyone or anything become an idol above God.

An intentional decision to live this way—emulating His divine characteristics with your human limitations—is a beautiful sacrifice to God. What a privilege to build your life to reflect His goodness, knowing it requires mindful choices every day. Choosing His way over what's trending delights God's heart. He calls that kind of living beautiful.

....

*Father, help me represent You well in my words and actions.
Give me courage to make the hard choices as I purpose to imitate
You in my life. My efforts will be imperfectly perfect, and I'm
grateful that's good enough for You! In Jesus' name I pray. Amen.*

A Beautiful Forever

The Spirit of God whets our appetite by giving us a
taste of what's ahead. He puts a little of heaven
in our hearts so that we'll never settle for less.

2 CORINTHIANS 5:5 MSG

Earth is a temporary location for your eternal soul. The body you live in today will not be the body you have for forever. And when you accepted Jesus as your Savior, God's Holy Spirit took up residency in your heart to prepare you for things to come. He puts in you a longing for your final destination—heaven. He gives you hope and a future. The Spirit stirs in you an excitement for what's ahead. And until that beautiful promise of living and worshipping in His presence is fulfilled, He gives you a love for the Lord and a strong desire to experience Him right now. Your ability to love God and long for a relationship with Him comes from the Holy Spirit in you.

Grab onto it, friend! Let that love grow deep and invest your time growing closer to Him. Embrace all the Spirit has to offer you every day, and be a bright light for the world to see. And when life feels too hard or scary, remember this life is a breath. You are passing through on the path to eternity with God. It's going to be more beautiful than you can imagine!

....

Father, I'm excited about being able to spend
eternity with You! In Jesus' name I pray. Amen.

You Are Fully Accepted

*And you did not receive the "spirit of religious duty," leading you back
into the fear of never being good enough. But you have received the
"Spirit of full acceptance," enfolding you into the family of God. And
you will never feel orphaned, for as he rises up within us, our spirits
join him in saying the words of tender affection, "Beloved Father!"*
ROMANS 8:15 TPT

It's so easy to feel like we're not good enough. We can feel it as daughters and mothers, as friends and employees, and in a million other nooks and crannies of our lives. It's a fear that often keeps us from embracing all God has for us because we lack the confidence to step out or try again. We struggle to feel worthy of love because the messages saying we are unacceptable and unwanted are overwhelming.

Sweet one, the world may not love you the way you want to be loved. Others may never see your awesomeness or appreciate all you have to offer. But let this truth sink deep into your heart: you're 100 percent approved of and accepted by God. He is completely delighted with you. And He will always call you worthy and beautiful, because that's who He created you to be.

*Father, sometimes I feel unaccepted by the world. What a relief
to know I am fully accepted by You! Thanks for loving me
the way You do. In Jesus' name I pray. Amen.*

Passionate Praise

You are my strength and my shield from every danger. When I fully
trust in you, help is on the way. I jump for joy and burst forth with
ecstatic, passionate praise! I will sing songs of what you mean to me!
PSALM 28:7 TPT

How would your life be different if you knew deep in your DNA that God
is your strength and shield and that His promise is to protect you? If you
really believed He was all the help you needed—that He was your source for
everything—how would you respond?

The psalmist breaks out into passion-filled praise! He sings his prayers to
the Lord, thanking and acknowledging Him for all He's done. He chooses to
surrender any fears or insecurities about what's ahead, and instead trusts
the Lord completely. Friend, let this be an encouragement. God is waiting
for you to embrace His promise of protection because He knows it will give
your heart a joyous reason to praise Him. And to God, that kind of response
to His love is a beautiful thing to behold.

....

Father, it's hard to let go and trust someone else with my life.
It feels unsafe. Help me know You are trustworthy and faithful.
Help me remember that You are active in my life. And, Lord, would
You give me the courage to surrender my cares and the confidence to
passionately praise You for helping me? In Jesus' name I pray. Amen.

A Beautiful Life

*There is nothing better than for people to eat and drink and to
see the good in their hard work. These beautiful gifts, I realized, too,
come from God's hand. For who can eat and drink and enjoy the good
things if not me? To those who seek to please God, He gives wisdom
and knowledge and joyfulness; but to those who are wicked, God keeps
them busy harvesting and storing up for those in whom He delights.
But even this is fleeting; it's like trying to embrace the wind.*

ECCLESIASTES 2:24-26 VOICE

The Lord wants you to enjoy life, and the ability to do so comes from Him. He wants you to enjoy the everyday things, like eating, drinking, being in community, and doing satisfying work. God's desire is for you to have a beautiful life, even in tough times. And choosing to include Him in those everyday activities—being deliberate about your relationship with the Lord—pleases Him more than you can know. It's because of that choice that He promises to bless you with wisdom, knowledge, and joy so you can live life to the full.

*Father, I want to live a beautiful life defined by my relationship with You.
Help me choose to enjoy my life, embracing the good and the messy in equal
measure. Let me stand in faith and be blessed for it. And let me be pleasing
in Your eyes. I am so grateful for You, Lord. In Jesus' name I pray. Amen.*

Bursting Bubbles

The bubble of human pride will be burst; the arrogant will be pulled down from their pedestals. Then, finally, the Eternal, no one and nothing else, will be the center of attention, lifted up in high esteem.

ISAIAH 2:11 VOICE

Have you noticed the explosion of self-promotion? From epic vacations to high-achieving kids to diet success, we live in a society where bragging about everything going right in someone's life happens on the regular. And it seems social media has played a big part in it. Done right, social media is a great way to keep up with family and friends, but many are using it as a platform to sing their own praises.

God is clear about His feelings on pride. He promises to burst the bubble of vanity and remove the arrogant from their lofty positions of self-importance. This warning isn't meant to be cruel, nor is it a call to be full of self-loathing or to refuse to share exciting news with others. Instead, it's a reminder that God deserves center stage. He should be the One receiving praise and glory. Choosing to keep that perspective delights the Lord, and He will call your humble heart beautiful.

....

*Father, help me never to boast in the good things You
send my way. You are the only One I want to boast in,
because You are the Giver of all good things. Help me keep
that perspective every day. In Jesus' name I pray. Amen.*

Unashamed

For the Lord GOD helps Me, therefore, I have not been
ashamed or humiliated. Therefore, I have made My face
like flint, and I know that I shall not be put to shame.
ISAIAH 50:7 AMP

Shame is a silent killer because it often operates without us even knowing. We may not understand why we feel so bad about ourselves, but we do all the same. We battle overwhelming feelings of being wrong or broken or unlovable. Shame whispers, *Who you are is not okay*, into the deepest places in our heart. It tells us that no matter how hard we try, we'll never be good enough. And because we don't understand what we're dealing with, we can't seem to find a way to escape these joy-draining thoughts.

Cry out to God for help, sweet one. Ask Him to reveal the shame and heal you from it. With His help, it is possible to live without self-loathing. His plans never included you battling feelings of self-hate. You are a delight to Him! So ask God for courage to reject the lies shame speaks. And ask for the determination necessary for you to choose to believe that the God who created you calls you beautiful.

. . . .

Father, please reveal and heal shame in my life. I'm tired of feeling
this way. And would You please remind me of my goodness in You?
I could use that reminder right now. In Jesus' name I pray. Amen.

You're His Beloved

*Consider the kind of extravagant love the Father has lavished
on us—He calls us children of God! It's true; we are His beloved
children. And in the same way the world didn't recognize
Him, the world does not recognize us either.*

1 JOHN 3:1 VOICE

The Lord loves you lavishly. There will never be anyone who cares for you more. It's not that they don't want to or don't try to; it's that no one has the ability to out-love God. Not your mom, dad, aunt, grandparents, spouse, boyfriend, children. Only God can give the kind of extravagant love we need to thrive.

He loves you so deeply because you are His child. You're His creation. You are made in His image, bearing His characteristics. Your Father carries pride for you in His heart, and He is always cheering you on! Even more, there is nothing you can do to make God love you more or less than He does this very second. He is crazy about you, and that's why He calls you beautiful. . .inside and out.

....

*Father, I needed to be reminded that I'm loved because sometimes
I feel so unlovable. It's hard to accept love because I feel so unworthy
of it. And while I may not always understand why You care for me the
way You do, I'm so very thankful! Your extravagant love humbles me.
And, Father, I love You right back. In Jesus' name I pray. Amen.*

A Closed Case

*So now the case is closed. There remains no accusing voice of
condemnation against those who are joined in life-union with Jesus,
the Anointed One. For the "law" of the Spirit of life flowing through
the anointing of Jesus has liberated us from the "law" of sin and death.*
ROMANS 8:1–2 TPT

Jesus' death on the cross made a new way. His blood bridged a gap. His sacrifice replaced the law with unending grace, which means when God looks at you. . .He sees perfection. Why? Because He looks at you through the blood of His Son. You are free from any condemnation. Jesus paid the price with His life so you could live in freedom.

So, friend, that means there's nothing in your past that keeps you from God's love. He isn't ashamed of who you are or what you've done. There's no current sin that disqualifies you or makes you unacceptable in His eyes. You cannot become unworthy to Him. And Jesus' redemptive work on the cross means you are liberated. While it may be hard to understand how a perfect God can adore such an imperfect woman, it doesn't change the truth that He does. Completely. When God thinks of you, He beams with pride at His beautiful daughter.

. . . .

*Father, thank You for Your Son and for the sacrifice made
to save me from condemnation. I may not feel deserving,
but I will always be grateful. In Jesus' name I pray. Amen.*

More Than Enough

And God is able to make all grace [every favor and earthly blessing]
come in abundance to you, so that you may always [under all
circumstances, regardless of the need] have complete sufficiency
in everything [being completely self-sufficient in Him], and have
an abundance for every good work and act of charity.

2 CORINTHIANS 9:8 AMP

You, beautiful one, were created to live and love others well. You were made to do good things, helping those in need and giving of your time and talents. We all have purpose, and ultimately it's to point those around us to the Lord. That's why God promises to provide all we need to be intentional to walk out the life He has chosen for us. And when we get to the end of our abilities and feel overwhelmed or exhausted by the task set before us, we can find an abundance of help from our heavenly Father. He promises to make us sufficient in Him and through Him. That means no work is too big or too hard when we lean on the Lord for wisdom and guidance.

Where do you feel unqualified? Are you ready to give up? Ask for His favor and blessing in those areas. Tell Him your needs and fears. He knows your beautiful heart and is ready to equip you with more than enough.

....

Father, I need Your grace to keep going. Please bless me
in abundance for this work. In Jesus' name I pray. Amen.

Lift Your Voice

*Compose a new song, and sing it to the Eternal because of the unbelievable
things He has done; He has won the victory with the skill of His right
hand and strength of His holy arm. The Eternal has made it clear that
He saves, and He has shown the nations that He does what is right.*
PSALM 98:1–2 VOICE

While you may have never seen God face-to-face, are you able to see His fingerprints on your life? Think about it. Can you remember impossible situations that worked out for the good? Have you seen unrepairable relationships find common ground again? Did a health issue resolve itself, confounding doctors? Did money show up right in the nick of time? God so loves you, and if you really watch for Him, you'll see Him everywhere.

Don't forget the value and importance of recognizing His intervention. The Lord is worthy of your praise! He has saved you, protected you, given you peace and wisdom, directed your steps, placed hope in your heart, filled you with joy, and loved you completely. Ask Him for eyes to see the ways He has shown up in your life. And then sing to Him! Speak out your gratitude. Because hearing your voice lifted up in thanksgiving is beautiful to His ears!

....

*Father, I can see You working in my life, and I am so grateful for it!
Thank You for loving me the way You do! In Jesus' name I pray. Amen.*

You Are Crowned Royalty

But You placed the son of man just beneath God and honored
him like royalty, crowning him with glory and honor.
PSALM 8:5 VOICE

The next time you feel ugly or unworthy or unloved, reread this verse. When you're depressed because you don't fit in or angry about your imperfections, find Psalm 8:5 in your Bible. Every time you start entertaining the lie that says you're not good enough or will never measure up, speak the psalmist's words aloud. Yes, there are plenty of people and circumstances that can make you doubt your value, but this verse tells it like it is. Friend, you are crowned royalty.

What are some measures you can put in place that will help remind you of this truth? Do you write it on your bathroom mirror in eyeliner? Maybe you scribble it on an index card and tape it to your car's dashboard. What about memorizing this powerful passage and speaking it out loud to yourself every day? Whatever needs to happen to help this sink into your DNA, do it. And never forget that God Himself, fully sovereign and in control, decided to crown you with glory and honor. He made you royalty.

....

Father, what a powerful reminder of who I am. You chose to make me
crowned royalty, and that means I have immeasurable value no matter
what anyone else thinks. Thank You! In Jesus' name I pray. Amen.

Pure, Proved, Perfected

O Lord, we have passed through your fire; like precious metal
made pure, you've proved us, perfected us, and made us holy.
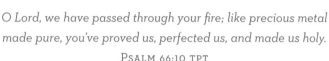
PSALM 66:10 TPT

Have you ever asked God, *Why me?* when you've had to face difficult situations? Maybe you've not only asked that question but also been angry with Him for allowing hard times and mean-spirited people into your life. Honestly, friend, that's a very normal response to life-changing and joy-draining moments. This world isn't a cakewalk. But the writer of today's scripture is demonstrating something important. The psalmist is sharing a shift in perspective that helps to make sense of things. It's choosing to zoom out to a 30,000-foot view and see the bigger picture.

God never wastes a thing. And the only reason He'd allow any sort of pain or heartache to intersect with your life is because His plans are to use it to purify, prove, or perfect. God uses everything for your benefit. So you can trust that God is fully aware of everything you're facing. He has complete understanding of every situation. And because He is so crazy about you, He will make all the pain produce something beautiful in you that nothing else could produce.

....

Father, I don't know how You do such amazing things,
but I'm so thankful You do. I appreciate Your
care and love. In Jesus' name I pray. Amen.

No One Is Better

*The rich and the poor shake hands
as equals—GOD made them both!*
PROVERBS 22:2 MSG

Do you ever feel inferior to someone else? Maybe you've decided they're prettier, more athletic, smarter, or have a nicer home. Maybe their clothes are designer, their car is loaded, and their vacations are lavish. Sometimes we give jealousy a foothold in our heart, especially when we listen to the lies that whisper, *Those people are better than you.*

Are you entertaining lies? Have you decided you're less than someone else? Who are the women (or men) you're comparing yourself to, and what—in your mind—makes them better? Take a minute to think about it. You may not even be aware you're feeling this way!

Now allow the truth of today's verse to sink in. God is clear that no one is better than anyone else. He made every one of us unique and special, each with our own set of challenges and celebrations. You don't have her life because you're not equipped for it. She doesn't have yours because it wasn't God's plan. The Lord doesn't see you as less than or better than. He looks at His wonderful handiwork and calls us each worthy and beautiful, *equally.*

....

*Father, I struggle with comparison even though I know it
steals my joy. It helps to know You created and consider
everyone equal, regardless of what treasures we have here
on earth. I love You for that. In Jesus' name I pray. Amen.*

Beautiful Surrender

*Laying your life down in tender surrender before the
Lord will bring life, prosperity, and honor as your reward.*
PROVERBS 22:4 TPT

Too often, we make life all about us. We become self-centered, always making sure we're taken care of. We promote self-importance, manipulating others to think we are superior. And we decide that everything we have and every achievement we've reached is because of our hard work, dedication, wisdom, and strength. Without considering that God is the source of all good things, we take all the credit.

But this approach to life will end up biting us in the backside, because God is a jealous God and He will not allow any god above Him—even when that god is us. He's clear about His feelings on pride throughout His Word. It's something He will not tolerate. But when we choose to recognize the Lord's hand in our life, He promises to bless us for making the right choice. Just as any good parent rewards their child when they obey, so does God. And when we forgo our need for recognition, God calls that surrender beautiful.

....

*Father, help me be humble. Bless me with eyes to see Your hand in
my successes, and help me be quick to give You the credit. It's really
not about me. It's about You! Help me live my life in such a way that
You are always the One glorified! In Jesus' name I pray. Amen.*

Be an Extension of Jesus

Do not cheat poor people just because they are vulnerable or use
shady tactics in court to crush those already suffering; for the Eternal is
ready to take their case, and He ruins anyone who is out to ruin them.
PROVERBS 22:22–23 VOICE

Jesus came to love others and show them a different way of living. Never once did He shy away from the sick or downtrodden. He didn't keep a safe distance from those society considered unclean. He didn't keep company exclusively with the rich. Instead, He sought out the vulnerable. He was drawn to the suffering. And He stood up for the unwanted, the unaccepted, and the unloved. His kindness changed their lives.

Choose to be like Jesus. In a world where you can be anything, decide to be kind. What a gift you can offer others by just being generous with your words and actions. Being the hands and feet of Jesus to the lost and hurting is an amazing privilege. Sometimes all it takes to encourage another is compassion. When you choose to live and love with benevolence, God sees that intentional choice to be an extension of His Son and calls it beautiful.

....

Father, it's not always easy to be kind. Sometimes my own hurt
and anger make me want to lash out. Give me the courage
to be kind no matter what. In Jesus' name I pray. Amen.

Exceeding Expectations

O Lord, our God, no one can compare with you. Such wonderful works and miracles are all found with you! And you think of us all the time with your countless expressions of love—far exceeding our expectations!

PSALM 40:5 TPT

What are your thoughts about God? Do you think He is kind and generous, always looking out for your best interest? Is He capable? Does He do what He says in His Word He will do? Is He who He says He is? Are you able to fully trust God, knowing He is faithful? Is the Lord good to you and to those you love? Or do you struggle to believe Him? Sometimes surrendering your worries and concerns to Someone you can't see with your eyes seems like a tall order. Maybe you're angry about losing a spouse or put out that He didn't answer your prayer like you wanted. Friend, it's okay if you are. He can handle your frustrations and fears.

But your feelings don't change the truth of who God is. Everything in this world changes except Him. He loves you unconditionally and cares about every single detail of your life. And if you choose to believe His love and watch for His hand in your circumstances, the Lord will exceed your expectations every time. His plans for you include a beautiful future full of hope!

....

Father, I'm choosing to believe You!
In Jesus' name I pray. Amen.

You're the Leading Lady

We stand to inherit even more. As His heirs, we are
predestined to play a key role in His unfolding purpose
that is energizing everything to conform to His will.
EPHESIANS 1:11 VOICE

Before the world was formed, God thought you up. He spent time coming up with a beautiful purpose for your time on earth. He decided the community that would surround you and the impact you'd have on one another's lives. God gave attention to when you would come on the scene and carefully equipped you and others for your grand entrance. In advance, He made you the leading lady in His plan and purpose for your life, which means you receive all the benefits and blessings that come with that role.

The world may be quick to tell you hurtful things to make you doubt yourself. Sometimes you may feel more like an understudy than a woman confidently leading throughout life. But none of that changes the truth. God is always in control as He guides you to discover and play out the key role made just for you. And it's your passion for the life He designed that delights Him!

....

Father, I just love You! What a privilege to be Your leading
lady in the life You created for me. Help me live it out with
passion and purpose! And give me confidence to make good
choices so I glorify You. In Jesus' name I pray. Amen.

A Heart Full of Care

And he has appointed some with grace to be apostles, and some with grace to be prophets, and some with grace to be evangelists, and some with grace to be pastors, and some with grace to be teachers. And their calling is to nurture and prepare all the holy believers to do their own works of ministry, and as they do this they will enlarge and build up the body of Christ.

EPHESIANS 4:11–12 TPT

God, in His infinite wisdom, has appointed a beautiful purpose for each of us. He wants us to help point others to Him. Our job is to encourage believers in their journey, to help them take the next right step. God's plan is that we work together in community to build one another up in faith to withstand the challenges that come our way. What a perfect reminder that we're not designed to do life alone. Going solo was never the plan.

Where could you be offering encouragement to others? It's important to watch for those who need help or hope, remembering that the Lord loves a heart full of care for others. We're in this journey together.

....

Father, thank You for appointing each of us to help nurture and prepare believers. Help me understand how I fit in and what I can do to help. And give me words of life so I can encourage those around me. In Jesus' name I pray. Amen.

Unquestionably Lovely

He has made everything beautiful and appropriate in its time.
He has also planted eternity [a sense of divine purpose] in the human
heart [a mysterious longing which nothing under the sun can satisfy,
except God]—yet man cannot find out (comprehend, grasp) what God
has done (His overall plan) from the beginning to the end.

ECCLESIASTES 3:11 AMP

What a potent reminder for the weary ones worried about fitting in and being loved. Let this be an anthem that resonates deep in your soul, revealing the truth of God's creation. Too often we let the world's condemning words make us feel ugly. We decide we're unacceptable because we look different than the trending beauty standards. We focus on our imperfections and become hypercritical of ourselves. And it leaves us feeling lousy.

But God is crystal clear on this subject. He tells us that everything He has made is beautiful. Everything. That includes you, sweet one. And while you may not be beautiful according to the world's rigorous measurement, you are unquestionably lovely to Him. Let that matter the most.

....

Father, I confess this is a hard topic for me because I struggle with feeling
good enough. Sometimes I want so desperately to be loved and accepted
by others. I want to fit in. But I don't want to be chasing acceptance when I
already have it in You. Please remind me. In Jesus' name I pray. Amen.

A Beautiful Choice

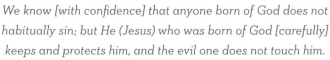

We know [with confidence] that anyone born of God does not habitually sin; but He (Jesus) who was born of God [carefully] keeps and protects him, and the evil one does not touch him.

1 JOHN 5:18 AMP

Every day, we have choices. Some lead us into a closer relationship with God, like being intentional to spend time in the Word, talk with the Lord regularly, gather in corporate worship, and surround ourselves with like-minded community. But other choices can cause us to push God away because we feel ashamed, unworthy, and disappointing. Jesus is the One who gives courage to make the hard choices. He is why we can take a stand for what we know is right and just. He is why we can confidently say no to sin.

Where are you struggling right now? Is a certain sin trying to keep you from living your best life of faith? Are certain friends promoting the wrong things instead of the right ones? Is there something you need to change so you can choose the better option next time? The Lord sees your heart and knows your mind, and if you ask, He will help you make beautiful choices. Be confident in His willingness to help you.

....

Father, I don't want to live with habitual sin because I know it separates me from You. Give me confidence and courage to press into Jesus for help. And please protect me from the enemy's schemes. In Jesus' name I pray. Amen.

Radiate with Hope

Now may God, the inspiration and fountain of hope, fill you to overflowing with uncontainable joy and perfect peace as you trust in him. And may the power of the Holy Spirit continually surround your life with his super-abundance until you radiate with hope!
ROMANS 15:13 TPT

Can you imagine what an encouragement you'd be to others if you actually radiated with hope? The truth is that life is hard, and it can drain every ounce of joy in a moment. It may be a rude comment, a piece of bad news, a broken marriage, a wayward child, or a health or financial concern. It doesn't take much to feel despair these days.

But God is ready to intervene when you need it. He promises to fill you with hope that things will get better and inspiration to keep you moving forward. He guarantees that you'll be filled to overflowing with limitless joy and find peace in the chaos as you choose to trust Him. And the Holy Spirit will encircle and encourage you as you navigate each situation. You will be a woman steeped in the Lord, unshaken by difficulties. And that, friend, is a beautiful sight.

....

Father, thank You that I don't have to let hopelessness prevail, because You promise to bring joy and peace and revelation right when I need it. Help me be quick to cry out Your name when the storms hit. You're really all I need. In Jesus' name I pray. Amen.

Credit God

*So it makes no sense for any person to boast in God's presence.
Instead, credit God with your new situation: you are united
with Jesus the Anointed. He is God's wisdom for us and more.
He is our righteousness and holiness and redemption.*

1 CORINTHIANS 1:29–30 VOICE

If every good thing comes from God, why do we so often take the credit our-selves? Why do we brag about our wisdom or bravery, talking like we mustered up these things on our own? Why do we point out all we did to meet the dead-line, accomplish the goal, and win the award? Rather than boast of the ways Jesus showed up and helped us, we hog the spotlight meant to shine on Him.

All we have comes from Jesus. All we are is because of Him. He is why we can access wisdom and discernment to make good choices. He is the reason we're now right with God and can be free from sin. And Jesus is the One who makes us holy. When we choose to recognize His role in our life and give Him the credit for every good thing, the Father sees that beautiful acknowledg-ment and is well pleased by it.

*Father, I don't want to boast in anything about my life,
but instead give the credit where it's due. Help me be
quick to recognize Jesus for every good thing. And thank
You for the gift He is in my life! In His name I pray. Amen.*

The Beauty of Choosing God

*But when I speak to you the next time, I will reopen your mouth,
and you will proclaim to them, "This is what the Eternal Lord has
to say." At that point, it's each person's choice whether to listen.
Some will listen; others will refuse because they are a rebellious lot.*

EZEKIEL 3:27 VOICE

Because the Lord loves us, He gave us free will. That means we have the privilege and burden of making choices for ourselves. We get to choose whether we follow God or not. It's up to us to decide if we obey the Lord's leading or just do what feels best in the moment. Without choice, we'd be nothing more than robots programmed to follow orders. God doesn't force us to be in a relationship with Him; it's His hope that we'd willingly want to be.

Where are you with God right now? Are you in rebellion, running away from Him in anger? Do you refuse to listen to His leading and do what your flesh wants instead? Friend, God is continually inviting you to be in community with Him. He only wants what's beneficial for His precious daughter. Your best interest is always His motivation. And when you decide to follow your heavenly Father daily, He calls that choice beautiful.

....

*Father, I don't want to live in rebellion toward You. Give me courage
to follow You no matter what. In Jesus' name I pray. Amen.*

The Need To Be Known

"Before I shaped you in the womb, I knew all about you.
Before you saw the light of day, I had holy plans for you:
A prophet to the nations—that's what I had in mind for you."
JEREMIAH 1:5 MSG

Something powerful happens in a woman's heart when she feels seen. When someone knows the way we take our coffee, the books and movies that make us smile, the snack foods we crave, and the words we need to hear, we're delighted. Realizing that our needs and wants are important to another makes us feel loved. It makes us feel significant. But sometimes we forget we're already completely known.

Scripture confirms this weighty truth. It says that God knew everything about you even before He placed you in your mother's belly. He knew every achievement you'd celebrate, every challenge you'd face, and how your heart would respond to both. God has always known your fears and insecurities, understanding them fully even when you didn't. And because He is the One who created all of the glorious complexities that make you, you, He can confidently call you beautiful both inside and out.

....

Father, it feels good to understand that my deepest craving to be known
has already been fulfilled by You. Would You please be quick to remind
me of this truth when I need it most? In Jesus' name I pray. Amen.

An Intense Desire

I will give them a new, intense desire to know Me because
I am the Eternal One. They will be My people, and I will be
their God because they will return to Me completely.
JEREMIAH 24:7 VOICE

Just as we have a desire to be known, God does too. He wants you to make time every day to be in His Word, to tell Him about your life, to ask for what you need, to thank Him for what He's done, and to watch for the ways He blesses you. God is eager to reveal Himself to you through scripture, nature, music, and a million other ways. And the Lord wants you to see Him as your source—the One who's able and willing to meet your every need.

Sweet one, who gets your time and attention? Where do you invest your heart? Who is it you work hard to know and love? Let it be God. Make Him a priority. Ask Him to give you such an intense desire to know Him that it drives you into His presence daily. What a beautiful way to love back the God who loves you completely.

....

Father, You're such a good Father and I want to spend time
getting to know You better. Would You put in me a longing
to deepen my relationship with You? Give me a craving for
Your presence in my life. In Jesus' name I pray. Amen.

You Will Not Fall

God is within her, she will not fall;
God will help her at break of day.

PSALM 46:5 NIV

While this verse was written about the city of Jerusalem, this truth stands for us too. When you accept the gift of Jesus and He becomes your Savior, the Holy Spirit takes up residency in your heart. He is there to guide you into a right relationship with God. And when you trust and rely on Him for direction, He will keep you from destruction.

Friend, God is intricately involved in every aspect of your life. He has complete knowledge of every situation you're facing right now. He sees your tears and heartache and understands the pain you're feeling. God knows those times you want to give up and gives you courage to stay in the game. He recognizes the things that trigger your insecurities and has the perfect antidote to calm your fears. The Lord has sympathy when you want it, hope when you need it, and love when you crave it. He is always with you, always available, and always willing. And because He sees the beautiful life specifically planned out for you, He will not let you fall.

....

Father, what a relief to know You have my back and that You'll
be there to protect me from people and situations trying to
derail me from Your good path. I'm beginning to understand
just how much You love me! In Jesus' name I pray. Amen.

Nothing To Fear

*Clothed in strength and dignity, with nothing to
fear, she smiles when she thinks about the future.*

PROVERBS 31:25 VOICE

Sweet one, there's nothing for you to fear. Reread today's verse out loud and personalize it by replacing the word *she* with *I*. Let this be your declaration—your anthem of courage as you march forward into an unknown future. When you're intentional to do life with God and trust Him with whatever comes your way, fear loses its hold on you. It is unable to rob you of the peace that comes from the Lord. You truly will have nothing to fear.

Ask God to clothe you in strength and a strong sense of self-worth. Ask Him to bless you with freedom to dream about the future without trepidation. Ask for unshakable confidence to do the next right thing even if it requires a huge leap of faith. Let yourself hope for good things and make plans with a courageous attitude. It's that brave femininity backed with bold faith that makes you a force to be reckoned with, and it's a beautiful thing to behold.

....

*Father, I confess that I struggle with fear and it often keeps me from
living my best life. Rather than trust You and believe that You will guide
me through life, I cower in worry. Please give me the courage I need to
smile at the future through the lens of faith! In Jesus' name I pray. Amen.*

A Tangible Display of Your Worthiness

But think about this: while we were wasting our lives in sin,
God revealed His powerful love to us in a tangible
display—the Anointed One died for us.

ROMANS 5:8 VOICE

While you were spending time on selfish pursuits and making life all about you. While you were focused on fitting in with the crowd rather than deepening your relationship with God. All those times you chose the fun things instead of the right things. And even as your heart craved earthly pleasures over heavenly promises, God loved you madly and knew He needed to create a way for you to be in right relationship with Him.

Here's the coolest part. He didn't wait for you to come to your senses and clean up your act. He didn't wait for you to become *better* or *repentant* before He intervened. Right in the middle of our messy lives, God sent Jesus. He sent His Son as a tangible display of His powerful love. Christ died for every sin—past, present, future. Because you mean so much to the Father, He was willing to sacrifice Jesus to ensure a beautiful eternity with you. He calls you worthy!

. . . .

Father, it's hard to understand the depth of love You have for
me that would make You send Jesus. I'm so grateful salvation
required nothing from me except humble acceptance of
His gift. Thank You. In Jesus' name I pray. Amen.

You're Never Alone

This is My command: be strong and courageous.
Never be afraid or discouraged because I am your God,
the Eternal One, and I will remain with you wherever you go.
JOSHUA 1:9 VOICE

Friend, God will never leave you. That's a power-packed truth to cling to every time you feel abandoned or rejected. Even people with the best intentions will fail us. Divorce happens. Families splinter. Friendships break up. Coworkers change jobs. And so often these broken relationships make us feel deserted by the ones we never thought would leave. We're left feeling unworthy and unloved. We begin to doubt our value. Our foundation is shaken because the loss feels overwhelming. And a horrible feeling of isolation leaves us disillusioned, discouraged, and distraught.

What a relief to know that God's presence is always secure. Scripture tells us over and over and over again that God will never walk away. He will remain with you wherever you go. Let that promise be a constant comfort. God looks at you and sees a woman of immeasurable value. You are worth His time. You are worth His attention. To the Lord, you are His precious daughter in whom He is delighted!

....

Father, what a good reminder that I am never alone. Even when
my earthly relationships crumble and people walk away, You're
unwilling to leave me alone. Thank You for seeing the good in
me and for loving me so well. In Jesus' name I pray. Amen.

You Will

Her teachings are filled with wisdom and kindness
as loving instruction pours from her lips.
PROVERBS 31:26 TPT

Sometimes we look at the Proverbs 31 woman from the Bible and freak out because we see her as perfect. We decide we don't have what it takes to live up to her standards of living and loving. Rather than study that passage, we skip right over it. But her life isn't unattainable, and knowing that perfection isn't an option, she gives us direction for righteous living.

Friend, you no doubt speak with wisdom. Maybe not all of the time, but you have hard-won wisdom to pass on to others. Being filled with faith means compassion is easily accessed. You may not love perfectly, but you do love with purpose and passion. The Holy Spirit in you is growing the fruits of the Spirit—love, joy, peace, patience, kindness, goodness, gentleness, faithfulness, and self-control—to be part of your everyday life. So while you may feel intimidated by the Proverbs 31 woman, God intentionally created you to be a beautiful blessing to those around you. And with His help and your heart, you will.

....

Father, it's good to know I'm made to be a blessing to others. Thank You
for reminding me my job isn't to be perfect, but to be purposeful to
show up for my life. I want to love the community around me well
and glorify You at the same time. In Jesus' name I pray. Amen.

Saturated in Prayer

Don't be pulled in different directions or worried about a thing.
Be saturated in prayer throughout each day, offering your faith-filled
requests before God with overflowing gratitude. Tell him every
detail of your life, then God's wonderful peace that transcends human
understanding, will make the answers known to you through Jesus Christ.

PHILIPPIANS 4:6–7 TPT

What does being saturated in prayer look like to you? Think about a stack of pancakes drenched in maple syrup or a plate of nachos covered by queso. Or maybe it's your favorite salad doused in ranch dressing or extra-buttery popcorn. Can you see it? What if you drenched your life in prayer like these foods? What if every single part of your life was covered by prayer and petition?

God promises that if we take everything to Him, we will reap great benefits. Our anxious heart will find peace. We will receive answers and direction. Our faith will grow as we choose to trust the Lord with every detail of our life. And God will look at our devotion and declare it beautiful.

Father, I confess I try to go it alone way too often. Sometimes it feels easier not to burden You with things that seem small and silly. But since Your desire is to know the details of my life, I'm going to share! Thanks for wanting to know even those things. You're amazing. In Jesus' name I pray. Amen.

A Beautiful Expression of Love

*Lord, I will worship you with extended hands as my whole heart
explode with praise! I will tell everyone everywhere about your
wonderful works and how your marvelous miracles exceed expectations!*

PSALM 9:1 TPT

Can you tell the psalmist is over the top full of joy? He is raising hands of
praise with a heart full of gratitude for what God has done in his life. Have
you ever had a moment like that?

Maybe your marriage was saved, or a broken friendship was salvaged.
Maybe you got your dream job, or the sellers took your offer on the home
you so badly wanted. Maybe you reached your goal weight, ran the mara-
thon, started the business, or got the publishing deal. We all have those
throw-your-hands-in-the-air moments of praise when we know God just showed
up in a powerful way and helped us achieve our heart's desires. Those times
are weighty reminders that God sees us, knows us, and often will exceed every
expectation we're clinging to.

The Lord loves a joyful heart! When you're intentional to see His hand
in your life and take the time to praise Him for it, He sees that as a beautiful
expression of your love.

....

*Father, I want to be as joyful as the psalmist. I want my gratitude for
You to be overwhelming. Would You give me eyes to see the ways You are
working in my life? Thank You for everything! In Jesus' name I pray. Amen.*

By His Grace

*Today I am who I am because of God's grace, and I have made sure
that the grace He offered me has not been wasted. I have worked
harder, longer, and smarter than all the rest; but I realize it is not
me—it is God's grace with me that has made the difference.*

1 CORINTHIANS 15:10 VOICE

God's grace has given you the ability to become who you are today. Yes, of
course you had to make hard choices. You had to say yes to the right things
and no to the wrong things. It was up to you to stay faithful, use wisdom, and
develop perseverance. You had to choose to accept God's help and not waste
it. You had to put in the time and effort to learn and grow. But it is because
of God's grace that you are who you are and where you are today.

Take a moment to think of all the ways God has helped you get here.
Think of all the ways you've grown and changed. How have you matured into a
woman full of compassion and sympathy for others? What were those touch-
stone moments when He changed your perspective on a situation? What
situations have softened your heart? What events have strengthened your
resolve? Sweet one, God has been at work in your life, making you into the
beautifully strong and caring woman you are today. Thank Him.

Father, thank You. In Jesus' name I pray. Amen.

Smoothing Out the Road Ahead

Place your trust in the Eternal; rely on Him completely; never depend upon
your own ideas and inventions. Give Him the credit for everything you
accomplish, and He will smooth out and straighten the road that lies ahead.
PROVERBS 3:5-6 VOICE

God promises that when you choose to trust Him completely, things will begin
to make sense. You will clearly see the right path for your next step. Too often,
we decide we know what's best. We think our ways are better because it's
our life to live. And rather than talk to God about every single detail, we make
our own choices and take credit for any successes.

But the Word is clear. It tells us to fully rely on the Lord rather than follow
our own thoughts and plans. God has the unique advantage of seeing our
situation completely, whereas our understanding is severely limited by the
human condition. God is all-knowing. When we ask Him to straighten the
path before us, He recognizes the bravery we show in trusting Him with an
unknown future. And God calls that kind of courage beautiful.

....

Father, sometimes I need reminding that my ways are not Your ways
and my thoughts are not Yours. Help me trust You in all things and seek
Your wisdom and direction. Help me trust that You have me. And help
me give You credit for the good in my life. In Jesus' name I pray. Amen.

Believe and Be Favored

*"Great favor is upon you, for you have believed
every word spoken to you from the Lord."*
LUKE 1:45 TPT

These words were spoken to Mary when she was pregnant with Jesus. Her cousin Elizabeth was affirming that it was Mary's belief and trust in God's words that sparked His favor on her life. And while this incident happened thousands of years ago, the same powerful truth is available to us today. When we make the choice to believe God and put our faith in Him, He blesses us.

What promise has God spoken to you? You've probably never audibly heard His words like Mary, but you have heard Him nonetheless. It may have been a scripture that leaped off the page, a song lyric that caught your attention, a sermon that hit home, or consistent and persistent messages. God is alive and active, and He absolutely speaks to you every day in a million different ways. Your job is to watch for Him and activate your faith as you trust and believe. God will affirm that brave decision and bring beautiful blessings for it.

....

Father, I want to believe You, but sometimes I struggle with trust. It's hard to let go of control. Would You give me the faith I need to be certain of what You say? I don't want to doubt You because I know You're a good Father. I just need Your help to walk this out. In Jesus' name I pray. Amen.

Your Gift to the World

Let love prevail in your life, words, and actions.

1 CORINTHIANS 16:14 VOICE

Deciding that love is going to be your motive for all things will richly bless those around you. So often we're met with anger from others who can't see how their words and actions are unkind. We have to deal with rude and cranky people who take out their frustrations on those around them. And rather than create community, many of us put up walls of protection so we don't get hurt. But with the Lord's help, you can change that.

God wants love to prevail in your life. Choosing to be kind supernaturally breaks down defenses in others. It softens their hearts. It gives them room to breathe. Compassion is a great weapon against negativity because it tells others they're worthy of being loved. Even when you must have hard conversations, choosing to infuse your words and actions with kindness is powerful. Living with this sort of intentionality is a beautiful gift you give the world!

....

Father, help me be a light to others. Let the words I speak and the things I do be full of love and kindness to those around me. Help me bring peace and joy into hard situations, and give me courage to love those who are hard to embrace. I know I can do this only with Your help, so I'm asking for it right now. In Jesus' name I pray. Amen.

Chaos Calmed

*Chaos once challenged you. The raging waves lifted themselves
over and over, high above the ocean's depths, letting out their
mighty roar! Yet at the sound of your voice they were all stilled
by your might. What a majestic King, filled with power!*

PSALM 93:3–4 TPT

What is chaotic in your life right now? Where are waves raging against you?
Where are you fighting for peace? Chances are, more than one area needs
God's calming hand. Between health issues, financial woes, messy relationships, difficult bosses, and the ups and downs of everyday living, you're likely
feeling overwhelmed somewhere. Life is no cakewalk, that's for sure. But what
a caring God we have, who knew we'd need His help on the regular.

Ask God to speak into your situation. His voice carries the final authority.
His words are full of power and bring forth what He declares. In those times
when life feels too hard, talk to your Father and tell Him what you need. If
you don't know, ask Him to intervene on your behalf. Asking for help is a
beautiful demonstration of surrendering to the One you trust the most. He
will always answer His beloved daughter.

....

*Father, I am in awe of the power You have to calm the raging
waters in my life with Your words. I'm so glad You are my advocate
and help. Remind me to ask for Your help when I am feeling
overwhelmed. I need You! In Jesus' name I pray. Amen.*

It's Your Time

*"If you stay silent during this time, deliverance for
the Jews will come from somewhere, but you, my child,
and all of your father's family will die. And who knows?
Perhaps you have been made queen for such a time as this."*
ESTHER 4:14 VOICE

Esther had a choice to make. Would she take a risk and speak up for what was right, or would she stay silent and hope someone else would do it? Would she fight through the fear or cower under it? Even knowing all it could cost, she realized this was her time. Her courage was remarkable.

Being brave is hard, especially when major risks are involved. Doing the right thing is rarely the easy thing. But God chose you to be on earth at this time for a reason. There is a purpose behind your existence here and now. And being faithful often means standing up and speaking out when you feel God's prompting. Friend, you were made for such a time as this! Don't let fear keep you from grabbing hold of your calling. When you feel the nudge to speak up, trust that the Lord will give you what you need to be His bold and beautiful daughter.

....

*Father, I don't feel brave. I feel scared. And I need Your help so I can do
what You're asking of me. Give me the guts and grit to embrace the truth
that this is my time to live out my faith! In Jesus' name I pray. Amen.*

Completed by Him

*And our own completeness is now found in him. We are completely
filled with God as Christ's fullness overflows within us. He is
the Head of every kingdom and authority in the universe!*

COLOSSIANS 2:10 TPT

You can't do it by yourself. As much as you may try to have it all together and be the best version of you possible, you simply don't have the ability to make it happen. You can eat clean and work out regularly. You can generously volunteer your time and be charitable to others. You can work hard and save diligently for retirement. And you can live a full and faith-filled life marked by love and compassion. But every bit of your effort still is not enough to make you complete. Every one of us needs God for that.

It takes a surrendering of sorts. We have to recognize our desperate need for a Savior. We must remember we have human limitations and require help from a limitless God. And that realization is a beautiful thing, really. It takes the pressure off us to be everything to everyone. Instead, we can embrace the beauty of a relationship with the God who gives us what we need to live and love well. He completes us.

....

*Father, what a relief to know it's not all up to me. That's a gift
in and of itself! Help me remember that You're the reason
I can live a full life. In Jesus' name I pray. Amen.*

No Cowardice, No Cringing

For God did not give us a spirit of timidity (of cowardice, of craven and cringing and fawning fear), but [He has given us a spirit] of power and of love and of calm and well-balanced mind and discipline and self-control.

2 TIMOTHY 1:7 AMPC

It's easy to give in when the going gets tough or to give up when things get too hard. It's common to walk away when a situation feels overwhelming. It takes strength to stand up to bullies, be they people or circumstances. But, friend, God didn't create you with a spirit of timidity. He never intended for you to be a coward, cringing at life's curveballs. Instead, God filled you with a spirit of power, love, and a sound mind. Girl, you can do hard things.

So stand up, because you are brave. You may have real moments of fear, but you can do what needs to be done anyway. You are a woman with true grit who can choose to trust even when you feel scared. And it's your choice to grab onto courage in the chaos that is so beautiful to the Lord. You've got this.

....

Father, thank You for the reminder that You make me brave! Because of You, I am powerful and can do hard things. Help me remember too, that I am backed by a powerful God who deeply loves me. In Jesus' name I pray. Amen.

Everyday Reminder

*Let the dawning day bring me revelation of
your tender, unfailing love. Give me light for
my path and teach me, for I trust in you.*

PSALM 143:8 TPT

Ask the Lord to remind you every day that He loves you. We all need to know we're worthy and valued. We need to be retold on the regular that we have purpose, that we are necessary, and that we bring goodness into the world. It's vital we have timely reminders that we're fully accepted as we are—stumbles, fumbles, and all. Why? Because the world is quick to beat us down and make us feel lousy. And unless we deliberately fill our minds with the truth, we'll be left feeling discouraged and depressed.

Friend, God is absolutely crazy about you! There is nothing you can do more or less to change how He feels about you in this very moment. His love for you is unfailing. Unwavering. Unshakable. Make sure you watch and listen for His sweet reminders every morning, because you'll need His reassurance to help you navigate each day.

....

*Father, this world is a beast that threatens my sense of self-worth
every single day. Help me remember that I am loved by You and I
cannot change that no matter how many mistakes I make. Thank You
for seeing my value through all my mess, and thank You for caring
enough to tell me daily. I need to know it. In Jesus' name I pray. Amen.*

Jesus Proves It

*For when the time was right, the Anointed One came
and died to demonstrate his love for sinners who were
entirely helpless, weak, and powerless to save themselves.*

ROMANS 5:6 TPT

In today's world, admitting that you're helpless in any situation is considered very uncool. Confessing any kind of weakness does nothing but mark you as an easy target, leaving you feeling unsafe or vulnerable. And choosing to share your fears about being powerless seems like the perfect setup for others to take advantage of you. So instead of being real, many of us spend a great deal of time and effort covering up what's really going on inside. Being honest just feels too dangerous to our hearts.

But God knew these realities, and rather than prey on your feelings of helplessness, weakness, and powerlessness, He sent Jesus to rescue you. He loved you enough to save you from yourself. You didn't have to pull it together or tidy up your messiness, because He saw right through it all. God has known all along that you are His beautiful creation. And He sent Jesus to prove it.

....

*Father, thank You for Jesus! Thank You for knowing me completely
and seeing the good in me. Thank You for second chances and third
chances. Thank You for being a loving Father who tends to the heart
of His beloved daughter. I love You too! In Jesus' name I pray. Amen.*

It's All Planned Out

"I know what I'm doing. I have it all planned out—
plans to take care of you, not abandon you,
plans to give you the future you hope for."
JEREMIAH 29:11 MSG

Sweet one, deep breath. It's time for you to know without a doubt that God's got you. It may not feel like it sometimes because life is crazy. Maybe everything feels too unpredictable and scary, and you can't seem to catch a break. You may be battling old tapes and messages from your childhood that continuously tell you you're worthless. You may go through seasons where you get sucker punched at every turn. But none of that changes the truth that God is intimately involved in every single detail of your life. And nothing has happened to you that He has not been fully aware of and only allowed because He planned to use it for your benefit and His glory.

God has a future planned for you, and He has filled it with hope for His beloved daughter. He promises to take care of you and never abandon you. He has thought everything through and knows exactly what will happen. And when you decide to believe God and cling to His promises through the hard times, He looks at you with the deepest delight and says, *"Well done, daughter."*

Father, I trust that You have my life planned out
and that it will be for my benefit and Your glory.
Let's do this together! In Jesus' name I pray. Amen.

Speak Up or Stay Quiet?

"GOD will fight the battle for you. And you?
You keep your mouths shut!"
EXODUS 14:14 MSG

Keeping our mouths shut can be a tall order, right? Sometimes we just want to spew hateful words toward someone who has hurt our feelings. We want to yell and scream at our offenders the mean-spirited thoughts running amuck in our minds. And while finding our voice to advocate for ourselves is good and right, we have to be careful we don't annihilate someone with our words instead. It's important to know when to speak out and when to stay silent.

What if you trusted that God was fighting this battle for you? What if rather than taking matters into your own hands, you stayed quiet so He could handle it? There are times it's appropriate to speak up, and there are times when keeping your mouth shut is best. Ask God what He thinks. Let Him direct your next move in the process. Allow Him to be your fiercely protective Father when needed, because not every situation requires you to share your thoughts. Sometimes God's desire is for you to keep your lovely lips praising Him rather than defending yourself.

....

Father, sometimes I just want to let others have it. I want to say the
hateful things I am thinking because it will make me feel better,
at least in that moment. Please give me wisdom to know Your
will for me in each situation. In Jesus' name I pray. Amen.

Unstoppable

No one will be able to oppose you for as long
as you live. I will be with you just as I was with
Moses, and I will never fail or abandon you.

JOSHUA 1:5 VOICE

Be encouraged, friend! This is a beautiful promise from the God who loves you with an everlasting love. He has a perfect track record of sticking with His children and helping them when it seems everyone else has abandoned them. When you accept Jesus as your Savior, God puts His Holy Spirit in you as a constant companion. His presence within you is permanent. And while you may walk away from Him or turn your back altogether, God will not abandon you.

Moses desperately needed the Lord as he lived out his calling to free the Israelites and deliver them from Egypt to the Promised Land. It wasn't something he could pull off on his own. And while you may never be asked to do something on such a grand scale, the calling God has designed for you will be a life-changing one. It will require His grace and favor. He promises never to leave you to do it alone. His love and presence are unstoppable.

....

Father, I love knowing that Your will always will be done. And I'm
encouraged knowing that You'll ensure no one will stop the work
You've ordained me to do. I'm all in, Lord, and I'm grateful You'll be
with me in this grand adventure. In Jesus' name I pray. Amen.

You Belong

That's plain enough, isn't it? You're no longer wandering exiles. This kingdom of faith is now your home country. You're no longer strangers or outsiders. You belong here, with as much right to the name Christian as anyone. God is building a home. He's using us all—irrespective of how we got here—in what he is building. He used the apostles and prophets for the foundation. Now he's using you, fitting you in brick by brick, stone by stone, with Christ Jesus as the cornerstone that holds all the parts together. We see it taking shape day after day—a holy temple built by God, all of us built into it, a temple in which God is quite at home.

EPHESIANS 2:19–22 MSG

Friend, you belong. You have a forever family. You cannot be kicked out or tossed away for messing up. You don't have to perform perfectly to be included. You're an important member of the family of God.

Maybe you've never had a place where you felt you belonged. Maybe someone broke a promise or walked away. Maybe someone turned their back on you or betrayed you, making it hard to trust that God won't. But here's a solid truth that requires faith to believe: God is crazy about you, His beautiful daughter, and you will always belong with Him.

Father, thank You for giving me a place to belong when no one else did. In Jesus' name I pray. Amen.

Beautiful To God

*We know that all creation is beautiful to God and there
is nothing to be refused if it is received with gratitude.*

1 TIMOTHY 4:4 TPT

You may not feel beautiful by the world's standards, but you're stunning to God. And it's not your outward appearance that makes you lovely to Him. He's proud of your compassionate heart for others. He appreciates your desire to bring His goodness into the world. God delights in the selfless things you do to care for those around you, and in the way you put servant leadership into practice. He admires the times you try to do the right thing even when it's the hard thing, and He loves when you share your frustrations with Him. Girl, you are a blessing back to the One who created you.

So the next time you feel unlovable or someone reminds you of the ways you don't measure up on the world's yardstick for beauty, remind yourself that to God all of creation is beautiful. And that includes you. Tell yourself again (and again) that the goal isn't to fit in, anyway. And ask the Lord to fill your heart and mind with the knowledge of how much He loves you.

....

*Father, sometimes I focus too much on what the world thinks rather
than on what You think. So it does my heart good to be reminded
that I'm beautiful to You. Help me settle in my heart that Your
opinions matter the most. In Jesus' name I pray. Amen.*

You're a Crown of Glory

*You will also be [considered] a crown of glory and
splendor in the hand of the LORD, and a royal diadem
[exceedingly beautiful] in the hand of your God.*

ISAIAH 62:3 AMP

It's easy to get down on yourself. Maybe it was a trip to the dressing room where the harsh lighting exposed your imperfections. It could have been a glance in the full-length mirror that made you cringe as you took a second look. Maybe it was trying on the jeans that fit fine last month, only to discover they're a bit snugger than you remember. Or maybe it was the critical words spoken to you (or by you) that play on repeat. Regardless of what it is that gets you down, you might find yourself stuck at the bottom of a self-pity pit that's hard to climb out of.

What if you opened the Bible every time you felt discouraged about the way you look to see what God has to say? His Word is chock-full of weighty reminders that you are beautiful to the Father. He considers you a crown of glory, a masterpiece, a royal diadem. He knows worldly beauty is fleeting and temporary, which is why He decided to make you beautiful from the inside out.

....

*Father, I am tired of feeling unhappy about the way I look.
Help me anchor my self-worth in the way You see me.
It's really all that matters. In Jesus' name I pray. Amen.*

Refocus on God

*Here's the one thing I crave from God, the one thing I seek
above all else: I want the privilege of living with him every
moment in his house, finding the sweet loveliness of his face,
filled with awe, delighting in his glory and grace. I want to live
my life so close to him that he takes pleasure in my every prayer.*

PSALM 27:4 TPT

What do you crave more than anything else? What is it that keeps you up at night because it's all you can think about? Maybe it's recognition for a job well done; maybe it's internet fame. Could it be a flawless figure or an enviable marriage? Do you want a home full of children, your own company, a life of travel, or a gaggle of girlfriends? We all have something that tops our list, something we work toward. So what's yours?

In the verse above, the psalmist is making a bold declaration. And his desire is a worthy one that brings with it noteworthy benefits. But it's challenging to walk out daily because it means we shift our focus away from earthly pursuits and onto our relationship with the Lord. Friend, let this be our craving. Let's refocus on Him and live with expectation of our beautiful future with Him.

....

*Father, I cannot wait to spend time with You in heaven. Help me
live here like I'm expectant for there. In Jesus' name I pray. Amen.*

You Are Heard

*Saying Your name, Eternal One, I called to You from the darkness
of this pit. Surely You've heard me say, "Don't be deaf to my call;
bring me relief!" So close when I've called out in my distress,
You've whispered in my ear, "Do not be afraid."*

LAMENTATIONS 3:55–57 VOICE

Have you ever stopped to realize that the God of the universe—the One who created the heavens and the earth—has His holy ear turned toward you? You matter so deeply to Him that just uttering His name gets God's attention. The Lord is never too busy to listen immediately to your cry for help, request for wisdom, plea for peace, or whisper for hope. The very moment you need Him, God is there. As a matter of fact, He knows you so completely that He knows your needs even before you do.

In a world of uncertainty, be encouraged to know you are loved by a God certain of your worth. He deeply desires a close relationship with you, His prized creation. You hold such immeasurable value in His eyes that He never takes them off you. You are seen and you are known. And you are always heard.

....

*Father, I am never alone because You promise to be with me
and meet my needs. I feel so unworthy, but nonetheless I am
so grateful. Help me remember that Your help is only one
thought or breath away. In Jesus' name I pray. Amen.*

Beautiful Moments of Praise

*I'm overflowing with your praise for all you've done,
and your splendor thrills me all day long.*

PSALM 71:8 TPT

There's something so beautiful about an attitude of gratitude. It's humility, a recognition of your need for someone else. It's allowing others to bless you rather than thinking it's all up to you. Gratitude makes no room for pride. It's void of self-promotion. And it deepens relationships with others because your thankfulness blesses them for blessing you. Always live with radical gratitude, friend.

Now take that same concept of appreciation and turn it toward the Lord. Be quick to acknowledge the ways He's alive and active in your life. Give Him credit for knowing the exact thing you needed at the exact right time. Tell Him why you're thankful and how He has impacted your life. Sing to the Lord with a spirit of gratefulness. Kneel before Him, humbly recognizing the ways He has saved you, strengthened you, restored you. Be full of awe and wonder as you recount His faithfulness. God loves to hear your beautiful voice in those moments of praise!

....

*Father, thank You! I see the countless times You've shown up and
supported me through the good times and the hard times. My heart
is full of gratitude for the times You intervened when I didn't even
know it. I praise You for being the loving Father I need every day,
and for blessing me with all good things. In Jesus' name I pray. Amen.*

The Beauty of Being Available

Beloved friends, what should be our proper response to God's marvelous mercies? I encourage you to surrender yourselves to God to be his sacred, living sacrifices. And live in holiness, experiencing all that delights his heart. For this becomes your genuine expression of worship.

ROMANS 12:1 TPT

This verse is a call for us to be available to God. Paul is asking us to put God first, surrendering our agenda for His. Sweet one, He made you for a beautiful purpose, and it requires obedience. Every time you say yes to the Lord, you give Him the space to reveal the next right step for you to take. You are essentially sacrificing your plans for His.

Think about it. Are you selfish with your time and desires? Is it more important to accomplish your to-do list than to follow God's leading? When you choose to be available to walk out the plans He has for you, you delight His heart. The deliberate decision to be accessible whenever He asks is a powerful expression of worship. And your willingness to be an instrument in the hands of God is a beautiful gift of surrender—one that doesn't go unnoticed. To the Lord, it's part of what makes you beautiful.

....

Father, I surrender myself to You. Whenever You need me to speak up, speak out, or just love on someone, I will obey. I'll choose to set aside my plans for Yours. In Jesus' name I pray. Amen.

Be a Daughter of Action

*Put the word into action. If you think hearing is what matters
most, you are going to find you have been deceived.*
JAMES 1:22 VOICE

The Bible is our road map for righteous living. It offers insight, challenge, affirmation, and hard truths designed to help us navigate our one and only life on earth. But too often, we don't put what we read into action. We may sit in a church pew every weekend and listen to a power-packed sermon, but we leave that good teaching behind as we walk out the door. We may sit in a small group once a week and chew on the Word with our girlfriends, but then we never put into practice the amazing things we learned. Hearing alone is not God's heart for us.

Be the kind of woman who takes the Lord's instruction seriously. This isn't a call to live it out perfectly. Thankfully, not even God expects a flawless existence for His daughters. Instead, hearing what God says and walking out His will with purpose and determination is what pleases Him. He loves when we show up every day, full of passion to follow Him.

....

*Father, help me be the kind of woman who puts into practice what
I learn from Your Word. I know it pleases You, and that's my motivation.
Would You give me wisdom to discern Your Word and courage to make
hard decisions as I live it out? In Jesus' name I pray. Amen.*

A Warning To Heed

"Very truly I tell you, whoever hears my word and believes
him who sent me has eternal life and will not be judged
but has crossed over from death to life."

JOHN 5:24 NIV

How many times have you heard someone warn of something, but you ignored it? Like when the server brings your meal to the table and lets you know the plate is hot, but you touch it anyway. Or when you're advised to avoid the highway because of an accident, but you take it rather than an alternate route and end up late to a meeting. The truth is that there's a bit of a rebellious streak in all of us. But Jesus' warning in today's verse is a matter of life and death. Literally.

God wants you to be with Him in heaven for eternity—a place He's excited to share with those who choose faith. He's so crazy about you, friend! Since the day you took your first breath, He has been relentlessly pursuing your beautiful heart. He knows your immeasurable value and wants to share His very best with you. Heed His warning, understanding it comes from a place of pure love for the daughter who delights Him.

. . . .

Father, I confess I have a rebellious spirit that often ignores warnings that
come my way. But I take this caution very seriously. I want to be with You in
heaven forever. Yes, Lord, I believe in You! In Jesus' name I pray. Amen.

A Beautiful Resolve

Truth's shining light guides me in my choices and decisions;
the revelation of your word makes my pathway clear.

PSALM 119:105 TPT

You are not here to navigate life alone. God knows life holds too many ins and outs and ups and downs for you to be left to figure things out on your own. It's not because you're incapable. God made you brilliant, friend! But it's because He designed every one of us to be in community—community with others and with Him. So consider it a big red flag when you're feeling like you have to do things on your own. He cares for His beloved too much to let you be isolated.

But of all the resources God has provided to support you, the most beneficial will always be His Word. You may have a fabulous mentor, great parents, and smart friends, but the Bible is the most powerful source of wisdom. It's like a light because it guides you as you're having to make tough decisions. It promises to illuminate the right choices to help you live your best life. And when you seek wisdom and discernment in its pages, God calls that kind of resolve beautiful!

....

Father, I confess I don't always go to the Bible for answers.
Instead, I so often make choices based on how I feel or counsel
I get from others. Starting today, I am determined to seek Your
Word above any other advice. In Jesus' name I pray. Amen.

Worthy of Great Gifts

*So if you, who are sinful, know how to give your children
good gifts, how much more so does your Father in heaven,
who is perfect, know how to give great gifts to His children!*
MATTHEW 7:11 VOICE

Sometimes we worry God is angry with us, that He's frustrated with how we're living our life. We fear God will unleash His wrath or withhold His great gifts from us. And when we're certain the Lord is full of disappointment, feelings of self-doubt can shake us to the core. We stop talking to God and quit asking for help. In the end, we often walk away full of shame and guilt.

But here is a powerful truth to settle in your heart today. God is not mad at you. He loves you regardless of how messy your life is, how bad your decisions have been, or how many mistakes you've made. He has endless and unshakable love for you, beautiful one. And as a proud parent of His beloved daughter, God knows you're worthy of His great gifts that He planned in advance to share with you!

*Father, You're the best Parent. Thanks for loving me even though
I can be a hot mess of bad choices. Help me not let shortcomings
keep me from asking You for what I need. I'm so grateful I don't
have to earn the gifts You have for me. Instead, You give them
to me because of Your love. In Jesus' name I pray. Amen.*

The Reason to Keep Your Cool

*Listen, open your ears, harness your desire to speak, and don't
get worked up into a rage so easily, my brothers and sisters.*
JAMES 1:19 VOICE

Few things are uglier than someone losing their temper and verbally berating others. The reality is that everyone gets angry sometimes. God created us with a full range of emotions. And honestly, people and situations can be so very frustrating. But often the best thing we can do is walk out James 1:19 instead of responding in the flesh.

What if you chose to listen, really listen to another's heart? What if you chose to keep your harsh opinions inside, refrained from defending yourself, and refused to make excuses for your behavior? This isn't being a doormat for others to walk all over. It's an opportunity to be a safe place for someone to open up about their hurts and frustrations. It's choosing to keep your cool rather than say something you may regret later. It's setting aside your pride and deciding to love. More than anything, surrendering your desire to react in kind is a beautiful gift to others that deeply pleases the Lord.

....

*Father, You want me to keep my temper in check—what a tall order! I want
to defend myself when I feel attacked, yet it's exhausting on so many levels.
I absolutely need Your help to make this work in my life. Please close my
mouth so I can be a blessing to others. In Jesus' name I pray. Amen.*

The Beauty of Obedience

*I just want to obey all you ask of me. So teach me, Lord,
for you are my God. Your gracious Spirit is all I need, so lead
me on good paths that are pleasing to you, my one and only God!*
PSALM 143:10 TPT

When you choose to obey God, even when it means taking a huge step out of your comfort zone, He is delighted. When you decide to follow His lead rather than take the path of least resistance, God smiles from ear to ear. Your willingness to do what He has asked—what you know is right—sets you up for His favor. Obedience may be difficult, but God will bless you for it.

Where are you struggling to follow His prompting? Is it forgiving someone who has hurt you? Is it walking away from a negative influence? Is it making changes to your lifestyle? Never forget God sees the sacrifices you're willing to make for righteous living. He understands the complexity of emotions you're feeling. He knows the tension between your choices. And the Lord is moved by your beautiful resolve to follow Him anyway. Well done.

....

*Father, I want to obey You, but sometimes it's so hard to choose it.
Give me the courage to say yes to You rather than taking the easy
way out. I need strength to walk out my daily decisions. I can't
do it without Your help. In Jesus' name I pray. Amen.*

That Pesky Stubborn Streak

I hear the Lord saying, "I will stay close to you, instructing and guiding you along the pathway for your life. I will advise you along the way and lead you forth with my eyes as your guide. So don't make it difficult; don't be stubborn when I take you where you've not been before. Don't make me tug you and pull you along. Just come with me!"

PSALM 32:8-9 TPT

We all have a stubborn streak. It's innate. We're born with it. Every one of us has a built-in rebellious spirit, especially when we're told we must do a certain thing. Think about it. Even if the next step is something you'd likely suggest, the fact that someone else suggested it first makes you want to protest. Are you giggling at this truth right now?

God is always for you, friend. Everything—every single thing—He does is for your benefit. As a loving Father, He's there to guide you down the pathway of the beautiful life He has designed for you. He wants to help you navigate it. But when you allow the stubborn streak space, it will do nothing but make life harder. What if, instead, you ask for the courage to go wherever God leads?

....

Father, I want that beautiful life. And I know it means I need to tame the stubborn streak. Help me find the confidence to follow Your lead. In Jesus' name I pray. Amen.

Surprise with Goodness

If you see your enemy hungry, go buy him lunch;
if he's thirsty, bring him a drink. Your generosity will
surprise him with goodness, and GOD will look after you.
PROVERBS 25:21–22 MSG

Every day, you have the privilege of finding ways to surprise others with goodness. You have the unique opportunity to care for others and treat them with kindness. Does someone need a meal? Do they need clothes? Do they need money? God considers your heart beautiful when you're willing to be an extension of His hands and feet.

How do you respond when prompted to be generous with your time and treasure? The truth is that oftentimes it's inconvenient. It usually requires us to step way out of our comfort zone. It causes us to rework our already packed schedule. And it calls for us to surrender our needs so we can attend to another's. But God is clear about His hope and expectation, and it comes with a powerful promise. God promises that when you are intentional to surprise others with goodness, He will be intentional to do the same for you. It's a win-win.

· ·

Father, I say yes to being your hands and feet toward others. I am all
in to help people in need. Please soften my heart to see their needs,
and give me the instant desire to surprise them with goodness. What an
honor to care for Your precious children. In Jesus' name I pray. Amen.

A God Who Comforts

Heavens, raise the roof! Earth, wake the dead! Mountains,
send up cheers! GOD has comforted his people. He has
tenderly nursed his beaten-up, beaten-down people.

ISAIAH 49:13 MSG

How are you today, beautiful one? Chances are you're feeling overwhelmed or underqualified. There is no shortage of those feelings. Or maybe you've been told you're unlovable by someone you trusted. Are you worried about something in your life that feels out of control? Have you been betrayed? Have you tried to fix a relationship that never seems to get better? Life has a special way of beating us up, doesn't it? Sometimes we feel like we'll never find peace. Or hope. Or joy.

Be encouraged today as you reread the verse above. God sees your pain. He sees all the ways you're hurting right now. He understands how you got here. And His heart breaks for His beloved. Your Father aches watching you struggle, and He never intended for you to do it alone. It's because of His unshakable love for you, His beautiful daughter, that He promises to bring comfort every time you need it.

....

Father, I need Your comfort right now. Things feel so hard
these days and I can't seem to catch a break. Would You
remind me that I'm lovable? Would You bring me peace?
I'm so desperate for You, Lord. In Jesus' name I pray. Amen.

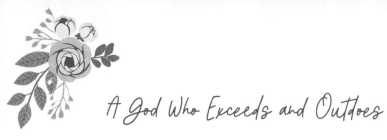

A God Who Exceeds and Outdoes

Never doubt God's mighty power to work in you and accomplish all this.
He will achieve infinitely more than your greatest request, your most
unbelievable dream, and exceed your wildest imagination! He will
outdo them all, for his miraculous power constantly energizes you.

EPHESIANS 3:20 TPT

Whatever it is you need from the Lord, He will exceed it. Any request you put before God will be the springboard for His plan to surpass every one of your hopes. The Lord wants the best for His daughters, and He goes above and beyond anything we may dream about.

Test this out in your own life. Make some time this week to allow yourself to daydream about something your heart desires. Write it down in a journal. Maybe it's a list of qualities you want in a spouse or a house. Maybe it's a far-fetched business idea or an open door to start your own business. Maybe it's a hefty fitness goal or lofty plans for retirement. Friend, God is inviting you to dream big, audacious things for your life. He loves your desire to create a beautiful and full life. So go ahead and dream, and then watch how He exceeds and outdoes.

....

Father, thank You for desiring to bless me in ways I've never imagined.
You love me so well, and I am humbled and grateful for it. I'm excited to
dream and watch what You do next. In Jesus' name I pray. Amen.

Your Beautiful Voice

At every time and in every place—from the moment
the sun rises to the moment the sun sets—may the name
of the Eternal be high in the hearts of His people.
PSALM 113:3 VOICE

Your praise is a beautiful gift to the Lord. When you are singing worship songs as you're driving to work, God smiles. When you recognize His hand in your situation and thank Him for giving you the strength you needed, He delights in your gratitude. When you cry out His name in the middle of a messy moment, He receives your plea with compassion. God loves to hear His name on your tongue. He loves to hear you in the good times and the hard times. He loves when you involve Him in your day. Your heavenly Father has a great affinity for your beautiful voice.

How are you walking out this verse well? In what ways can you do better? God is always waiting to hear from you, and He's available twenty-four hours a day, seven days a week. You don't have to make an appointment or wait in line. God loves you, friend. He is proud of His beautiful daughter. And He's listening for your voice.

Father, knowing You are always listening for
my voice makes me feel so loved. Thank You for
always being available. In Jesus' name I pray. Amen.

Beautiful Warrior

"I, even I, am he who comforts you. Who are you that you
fear mere mortals, human beings who are but grass...?"
ISAIAH 51:12 NIV

Fear is a big deal. And fear of man is something we all battle from time to time. We worry that others won't like us or won't take us seriously. We worry they will treat us unfairly or ruin our reputation. We're concerned about making someone angry if we speak our mind, or dealing with the consequences if we don't. For many, fear of what may happen at the hands of mankind is a constant companion that bullies us and steals our joy.

When those fears get out of control, let God be the One to comfort you. Let Him be the One to build up your confidence. The Lord will infuse you with courage to stand up for yourself so that others don't have power over you. He knows the beautiful warrior inside you because He put that confident spirit in your DNA. He made you to stand strong. And in those times fear feels too real, ask God to remind you of the warrior you are.

....

Father, I confess that fear gets too much playtime in my
mind. I am scared of what others may think of me or do to
me way too often. In those times, would You please help
me remember who I am? In Jesus' name I pray. Amen.

A Wall of Bronze

They will come at you, but I will make you like a wall of
bronze against them. They will not beat you, because I am with
you to save and rescue you. This will be so, for I have declared it.
JEREMIAH 15:20 VOICE

In this world, you will have trouble. Not new news, eh? The problem is that sometimes we are surprised that bad things happen. We're surprised that life isn't smooth sailing. And many believe that being a Jesus-girl means you will be spared from heartache, disappointment, and discouragement. But that's not theologically sound at all. As a matter of fact, you won't be spared from those things. You've dealt with all of them. And that won't change. The Lord, however, has made you a promise.

Even when it all seems too heavy and you feel cornered by enemies, God won't allow them any kind of victory. He will be there every moment of the battle and will keep you from losing. He will always rescue His beloved. He will save you from destruction. God loves His beautiful daughter and has firmly declared that you will be able to stand strong against whatever comes your way.

Father, protect me from those who want to hurt me. Keep me safe from the
ones who want to beat me down. I trust You to rescue me. And what a gift
that You've declared it in Your Word! In Jesus' name I pray. Amen.

Your Way May Not Always Be the Right Way

You may think you're right all the time,
but God thoroughly examines our motives.
PROVERBS 21:2 TPT

Of course, everyone wants to think they're right all the time. We desire the truth and pursue all the good things for us and those we love. We may be highly educated women with loads of life experience. While we may not have graduated from college, we most certainly have a degree from the school of hard knocks. And that has afforded us some hard-won wisdom. Not only that, but we've also watched and learned from others. We've journeyed through tricky times with friends, helping them navigate through the mess. We have read our share of helpful books and studied God's Word. But, sweet one, all these nuggets of wisdom don't always make us right.

Without a doubt, the Lord loves your beautiful desire to help others. He admires your fierce loyalty in walking through hard times with those you care for. And while you've collected valuable nuggets of wisdom along the way, God's hope is that you'll be humble enough to know your way may not always be the right way.

....

Father, help me set aside my pride so I am able to hear Your
heart for me. Give me the freedom to be wrong without feelings
of condemnation. And give me Your wisdom so I can live a
full and joy-filled life. In Jesus' name I pray. Amen.

Spending Time with God

Arise, my darling! Come quickly, my beloved. Come and be
the graceful gazelle with me. Come be like a dancing deer
with me. We will dance in the high place of the sky, yes, on the
mountains of fragrant spice. Forever we shall be united as one!
SONG OF SONGS 8:14 TPT

One of God's greatest desires is that you'll want to spend time with Him. You're His prized creation and He's interested in every single part of your life. He wants to know about what delights your heart, what makes you feel insecure, what pumps you up, and what causes you to feel fearful. You matter to God. You're His treasured possession. And while He already knows everything about you, God wants to hear your voice speaking and singing directly to Him.

It's your heart for Him that He finds so beautiful. It's the fact that you're willing to make time for Him in your busy day. It's that you seek God out when you need to vent about a heartache or squeal about a victory. And rest assured anytime you reach out to Him, God will be right there waiting.

....

Father, I never realized how much You want to spend time with me.
Your interest in me makes me feel so valued, especially because the world
doesn't always make me feel that way. Starting today, I commit to spending
time with You regularly, and I can't wait. In Jesus' name I pray. Amen.

Worth the Effort

I will personally gather the remnant of My sheep from the lands where I have driven them. I will bring them back to their home pasture where they will be fruitful and multiply. I will appoint new, responsible shepherds to take care of them, and My sheep will no longer have to be afraid. These new, responsible shepherds will make sure that none of My sheep go missing.
JEREMIAH 23:3-4 VOICE

This world does a good job of beating us up and making us feel we're an inconvenience. It tells us we're annoying when we try to advocate for ourselves. It reminds us that our needs are a nuisance, and our requests for help are a hassle. It makes us think we have to handle everything on our own because we're too messy. We're full of too much drama. And when we try to share our heart, it's often perceived as an annoyance.

But God doesn't feel that way. To Him, you're always worth His time and effort. He'll do the things that need to be done to care for you. You're never a bother or burden. Nothing about you is an inconvenience. Your broken heart isn't a frustration. He looks at you and sees His beautiful, treasured daughter. The world may be quick to tell you differently, but to the Lord you're always worth the effort.

....

*Father, thank You for knowing my worth and
making sure I do too. In Jesus' name I pray. Amen.*

The Beauty of Coming Alongside

All praises belong to the God and Father of our Lord Jesus Christ.
For he is the Father of tender mercy and the God of endless comfort.
He always comes alongside us to comfort us in every suffering so that
we can come alongside those who are in any painful trial. We can
bring them this same comfort that God has poured out upon us.

2 CORINTHIANS 1:3-4 TPT

Every time God comforts you, His comfort has a dual purpose. Not only is He committed to caring for His beloved daughter, but He knows it's also equipping you to help others walk through their own pain and trials. A beautiful depth is created in us every time we face dark times and come out the other side stronger. It forges the kind of compassion that enables us to understand what others are dealing with in their own lives.

Is there someone who needs your comfort right now? Maybe they've experienced unexpected loss or are walking through the many stages of grief. Is someone trying to heal from betrayal or abandonment? Life is full of pain points, and because God has comforted you through them, you're now equipped to help others. It's the beauty of coming alongside another.

....

Father, I never realized that the times You comforted
me were also the times You taught me to comfort
others. Thank You! In Jesus' name I pray. Amen.

A Heart of Contrition

God designed us to feel remorse over sin in order to
produce repentance that leads to victory. This leaves us
with no regrets. But the sorrow of the world works death.
2 CORINTHIANS 7:10 TPT

Have you ever done something that you knew was against what God wanted for you, and then felt guilty? Maybe there was a check in your spirit. Maybe it was a gut feeling that the choice you just made was the wrong one, and you couldn't shake it. These responses to sin are full of purpose. They are from God. They're not meant to beat you up, but rather to tender your heart toward repentance.

Are there choices you've made that you need to confess to God and ask His forgiveness for? Are you in the middle of a season of sinning that's making you feel contrite, knowing it's not God's best for you? The Lord finds a heart of contrition beautiful because it always leads to restoration. He will never hold your shortcomings against you. He'll never throw them back at you. And He promises that you will find freedom from the guilt and thrive without regret.

....

Father, I confess that I've been making some bad decisions lately
that I know don't glorify You. I'm thankful for remorse because
it's a reminder that I need to be more aware of my choices.
Help me be wiser in the future. In Jesus' name I pray. Amen.

He Comes to You

The one I love calls to me: Arise, my dearest. Hurry, my darling.
Come away with me! I have come as you have asked to draw you
to my heart and lead you out. For now is the time, my beautiful one.

SONG OF SONGS 2:10 TPT

When you cry out to the Lord, He hears you and responds with His holy presence. In those times you need the comfort only God can provide. He is right there. God draws close to you anytime you need His help because you are His beautiful daughter with whom He is well pleased. You may feel alone and abandoned, but you never are. He will never leave you. He'll never forsake you. You matter too much, friend.

In those lonely moments when you need to be reminded that you have significance, pray. Ask the Lord to fill you with a sense of His approval. Tell Him about the burdens of your heart, and invite His comfort and healing. God adores you and will not let you down.

....

Father, there are times I need to feel Your presence more than other times.
There are moments when You are the only One who can give me what I
need. Help me remember to ask You to draw near me rather than letting
myself be discouraged about my situation. In Jesus' name I pray. Amen.

The Giver of Joy

Gaze upon him, join your life with his, and joy will come. Your faces will glisten with glory. You'll never wear that shame-face again.

PSALM 34:5 TPT

When you feel that joy is gone from your life, take a moment to consider the state of your relationship with God. Think about whether you're focusing on the tough situation you're facing or rather focusing on the Lord. When you're intentional to make God number one and try to connect with Him regularly, the troubles of the day lose power over your heart. The people or circumstances that steal your joy lose their grip on your thoughts. Your faith is activated, and you gain an eternal perspective on life.

It's possible to be walking through extremely difficult times and still have a smile on your face. You can be in a pit financially and still have hope. You can be in a challenging relationship and continue living with joy. But a positive outlook in the midst of life's hardships is only possible with God. So ask for His help, beloved. To Him, holding on to joy in the midst of hardship makes you beautiful and bold.

....

Father, joy is hard to have when life kicks me in the gut. I need You to give me a holy perspective so I can walk with courage and hope. Be big in my life right now, Lord! In Jesus' name I pray. Amen.

He Made You Inside and Out

You formed my innermost being, shaping my delicate inside and my intricate outside, and wove them all together in my mother's womb.

PSALM 139:13 TPT

The Lord created you inside and out. He decided what color your hair would be and how tall you'd end up. He chose every feature that would stand out to make you unique from everyone else. God formulated your personality and quirks, your characteristics and creativity, and your talents and compassion. You weren't just another human to God. He took His time to make you a beautiful and cherished daughter. And because He's perfect in every way, He is incapable of making anything less than perfect. You're the way you are because He wanted you to be that way.

Hold on to this truth when the world tells you you're not good enough. Remember you were designed on purpose and for a purpose. Whenever you feel less than others who are always reminding you of any shortcomings, take a step back, take a deep breath, and think back over today's scripture. No matter what anyone says, you are an intentional creation and God is well pleased with His masterpiece.

....

Father, help me remember who I am through Your eyes in those moments I feel worthless in the eyes of others. Give me a sense of value, and remind me of my beauty. It's hard to hold that truth tightly sometimes, and I'm desperate for Your help. In Jesus' name I pray. Amen.

Every Single Moment

Every single moment you are thinking of me! How precious and wonderful to consider that you cherish me constantly in your every thought! O God, your desires toward me are more than the grains of sand on every shore! When I awake each morning, you're still with me.

PSALM 139:17–18 TPT

In those moments when you feel forgotten, remember that your Father in heaven thinks about you every single moment. You may feel overlooked and disregarded, but never by God. There may be times you feel completely alone and left to navigate life by yourself, but that's not the truth of things. Maybe those around you have turned their backs on you, but the Bible offers countless reminders that the Lord has never and will never follow suit. Sweet one, you are constantly cherished in His thoughts. You matter to God more than there are words to explain it. Others may not be able or willing to make you a priority, but to Him there is no other possible place for His beautiful daughter to be.

Where are you feeling unimportant? Where are you struggling to feel seen by those around you? Tell God everything. Open up and share your struggles right now. Let Him hear your heart so He can heal it.

Father, this truth is overwhelming and powerful.
Thank You for always loving me and never leaving me.
I'm so grateful I have You! In Jesus' name I pray. Amen.

Prepared and Spared

*You've gone into my future to prepare the way, and in kindness
you follow behind me to spare me from the harm of my past.
With your hand of love upon my life, you impart a blessing
to me. This is just too wonderful, deep, and incomprehensible!
Your understanding of me brings me wonder and strength.*

PSALM 139:5–6 TPT

Your future isn't left to chance. God would never allow that for His beautiful daughter. Instead, He thought ahead and planned out a future that would provide challenges and celebrations. It was all part of your creation, and God made sure to equip you for what He lovingly and intentionally designed. He has gone before you. But it gets even better.

In His loving-kindness, He also follows behind you to make sure your past decisions and choices don't harm what's ahead. God is intricately involved in making sure that His plans for you come to fruition. He has prepared and spared your beautiful future and promises to guard it. What a loving Father!

*Father, You've thought of everything. I can't even begin to under-
stand how You do it all, but I'm so thankful for the ways You love
and protect me. You're a good, good Father and I love You with all
my heart. Help me trust You as I make decisions and choices about
the next right step in my life. In Jesus' name I pray. Amen.*

A Beautiful Invitation

*God, I invite your searching gaze into my heart. Examine me
through and through; find out everything that may be hidden
within me. Put me to the test and sift through all my anxious cares.
See if there is any path of pain I'm walking on, and lead me back to
your glorious, everlasting ways—the path that brings me back to you.*

PSALM 139:23-24 TPT

What a beautiful gift you give the Lord when you invite Him into your life. It's choosing to surrender your innermost self but knowing the One you're inviting in is trustworthy. It's radical faith. It's epic faith. It's desiring above all else to fully share yourself with the One who created you. To God, this decision to surrender speaks volumes about the depth of your relationship. And it's beautiful.

Trust God enough to invite Him into the deepest places in your heart. Let Him reveal new and necessary truths to you. Choose to believe God will lead you back to Him because His heart for you is always good. His love for you is everlasting. And without a doubt, He calls you beautiful.

....

*Father, I willingly invite You into my life in significant ways.
I fully trust that You will be kind and loving, and I believe that
Your heart for me is good! Show me what I need to know. Lead me
where I need to go. I'm listening. In Jesus' name I pray. Amen.*

The Promises Attached to Suffering

And then, after your brief suffering, the God of all loving
grace, who has called you to share in his eternal glory in Christ,
will personally and powerfully restore you and make you stronger
than ever. Yes, he will set you firmly in place and build you up.

1 PETER 5:10 TPT

It's good to remember suffering is part of the human experience. No one gets a free pass to escape life's hardships. Everyone walks through seasons of darkness when they battle hopelessness. And if someone's life looks easy, it isn't. You may not get a front row seat to their tribulations, but that doesn't mean they don't have them.

But because God loves you so much, He has made powerful promises that make suffering palatable. The first is that suffering is short-lived. It's not forever, so hang on. And the second is that the Lord promises He'll give you strength through trials and make everything right in the end. So, friend, trust God regardless of what comes your way. And know that He calls that kind of faith beautiful.

....

Father, I know that any suffering I face is only because it will benefit me
and glorify You. Give me the courage to stay strong with unwavering faith
that You will work all things out in the end. And thank You for allowing me
to share in the sufferings of Your Son. In Jesus' name I pray. Amen.

Rejected To Accepted

But you are the ones chosen by God, chosen for the high calling of priestly work, chosen to be a holy people, God's instruments to do his work and speak out for him, to tell others of the night-and-day difference he made for you—from nothing to something, from rejected to accepted.

1 Peter 2:9–10 MSG

You're not who the world has said you are. Your value isn't based on the size of your jeans or the number on the scale. You aren't insignificant or unimportant because of your age, your education level, your skill set, your income, or your marital status. Others cannot accurately label you based on your skin color, hair color, or colorful past. The world's criteria are unfair and unbalanced, and it's an ever-changing measuring system of discouragement. Don't let the world define you, friend. Instead, believe you are who God says you are.

He has chosen you to be holy. He has created a beautiful purpose for your life that only you can walk out well. God has given you the ability to work on His behalf, pointing others to Him through your words and actions. And most importantly, the Lord has lifted you up above earthly rejection and reminded you of your eternal acceptance. You're His beautiful creation, and nothing can ever change that.

....

Father, help me reject what the world says about me and instead choose to see myself the way You do! In Jesus' name I pray. Amen.

Your Home Is Heaven

But there's far more to life for us. We're citizens of high heaven!
We're waiting the arrival of the Savior, the Master, Jesus Christ,
who will transform our earthy bodies into glorious bodies like his own.
He'll make us beautiful and whole with the same powerful skill by
which he is putting everything as it should be, under and around him.

PHILIPPIANS 3:20–21 MSG

Just hang on, friend. It's no secret that life is hard, and sometimes it takes all we have to get up in the morning and face the day. We all know nothing is fair and we'll face many trials and tribulations along the way. There may be people we deal with on the regular who can be mean-spirited for sport, trying to beat us up at every turn. Our health may turn on a dime and leave us grieving for what was. Finances may be a constant concern as we try to make ends meet every month. While life is filled with so much goodness, it's also filled with tremendous difficulties.

God wants to remind you this is not your home. It's not your final destination. And because you're a Jesus-girl, you'll spend eternity in heaven with the Lord. You'll have a new body untouchable by the effects of the world. And it will be beautiful.

....

Father, thank You for the reminder to hope in what's to come,
for here and now is temporary! In Jesus' name I pray. Amen.

Risky Business

"Not only that—count yourselves blessed every time people put you down or throw you out or speak lies about you to discredit me. What it means is that the truth is too close for comfort and they are uncomfortable. You can be glad when that happens—give a cheer, even!—for though they don't like it, I do! And all heaven applauds. And know that you are in good company. My prophets and witnesses have always gotten into this kind of trouble."

MATTHEW 5:11-12 MSG

Following God comes with risks. It sets you up to be ridiculed and made fun of. Just declaring that you're a Jesus-girl means bad things will probably be said about you. Some people may deliberately try to hurt your feelings and make you feel silly and insignificant. Lies may be spread and rumors started. This world is filled with hateful people who have strong opinions and a compulsion to harshly share them. But God's message to you is clear: Don't be discouraged.

What it means is that you're living in a way that points out God to others. Good for you! Well done! It means that your heart for Him is apparent. And, bold one, all of heaven is cheering you on as you choose to live your faith out loud. Your decision to be a woman of faith is beautiful in the Lord's sight.

....

Father, I'm not ashamed of the Gospel!
In Jesus' name I pray. Amen.

Be a Light

"Here's another way to put it: You're here to be light, bringing out the God-colors in the world. God is not a secret to be kept. We're going public with this, as public as a city on a hill. If I make you light-bearers, you don't think I'm going to hide you under a bucket, do you? I'm putting you on a light stand. Now that I've put you there on a hilltop, on a light stand—shine! Keep open house; be generous with your lives. By opening up to others, you'll prompt people to open up with God, this generous Father in heaven."

MATTHEW 5:14–16 MSG

Ever wonder what your purpose on earth is? Ever been confused about what God wants you to do with your life? While we've all been called to different stations of promoting the Gospel based on our God-given talents and strengths, there's one common thread. We are to be a light.

Today's verse is a weighty reminder to live your faith out loud. Don't hide the fact that you're a Jesus-girl. Don't be ashamed to pray in a restaurant or sing your favorite praise songs at the top of your lungs. God doesn't want you to tuck Him away. Instead, He loves to see you be generous with your life, telling others where He has shown up. Shine Him into the world!

Father, help me be bold in sharing my faith!
In Jesus' name I pray. Amen.

Powered by God

Who can find a truly excellent woman? One who is superior in all
that she is and all that she does? Her worth far exceeds that of
rubies and expensive jewelry. She inspires trust, and her husband's
heart is safe with her, and because of her, he has every good thing.
PROVERBS 31:10–11 VOICE

Many of us read scriptures like this and roll our eyes, certain we'll never measure up. We think this kind of woman is fictional, unattainable. And rather than dig in to see if there is anything in this verse for us, we skip right over it. But when we do, it's because we're forgetting one very important thing.

This Proverbs 31 woman is powered by the Lord. Because all good things come from Him, we can be sure of it. She may sound perfect, especially when we read that she's *superior* in all she is and does, but she battles the same human condition that we do. She probably has tons of help in the home while we end up frazzled trying to do it all. We may never fully know the hows and whys this side of heaven, but here's the takeaway: Asking God to empower you is not only wise; it's also a beautiful request to the Giver of all good things.

....

Father, please give me everything I need to
love my friends and family well. I can't do it
without You. In Jesus' name I pray. Amen.

Never Forgotten

*"Can a mother forget the infant at her breast, walk away from
the baby she bore? But even if mothers forget, I'd never forget
you—never. Look, I've written your names on the backs of my
hands. The walls you're rebuilding are never out of my sight."*
ISAIAH 49:15–16 MSG

There are some seasons in life when we feel overlooked and forgotten. Maybe the other person was chosen for the promotion instead of you. Maybe your husband is disengaged at home because his work is demanding everything he's got right now. Maybe you saw pictures of your friends on social media and realized you didn't get invited to a girls' night out. Or maybe it's just been awhile since someone asked to hang out with you. These times have a special way of making you feel unloved and unnoticed.

God is asking you to remember a big truth in those moments. He knows it's easy to throw a pity party and feel sorry for yourself. But He wants you to know you are beautiful to His heart and worthy of knowing that He has written your name on His hand. And while you may feel forgotten, you're not. Not only is your name written on His hand; you're also always on His mind.

....

*Father, it does my heart good to know I matter so much to You.
Help me hold on to that truth when I feel overlooked by others,
knowing I'm never overlooked by You. In Jesus' name I pray. Amen.*

Filling The Deficit

"I will be a true Father to you, and you will be my beloved
sons and daughters," says the Lord Yahweh Almighty.

2 Corinthians 6:18 tpt

Many of us had hard-to-love fathers growing up. Maybe it's because our fathers had the same. Maybe we didn't even have a dad because he died, or our parents divorced and he stepped out of the picture. It could be that the one we had was overworked at his job or under-committed in his home and wasn't involved or available. Maybe you're one of the blessed ones who had an amazing dad and you're still his little princess. Think about it—what was it like for you? What kind of dad did you have?

Isn't it just like God to see a possible deficit and step in? The Lord loves you enough to fill any gap your earthly dad may have left. And it's a privilege He takes seriously. That means He is always there for you, to listen, give wisdom, offer hope, extend strength. He's so proud of you, His beautiful and worthy daughter. So let God into your life in significant ways, and have confidence that your heavenly Father will meet any and every need that comes your way.

....

Father, please heal the pain left by my dad. Help me remember
You'll be with me every step of the way as I navigate the
ups and downs of life. In Jesus' name I pray. Amen.

A Beautiful Friendship

"I have never called you 'servants,' because a master doesn't confide in his servants, and servants don't always understand what the master is doing. But I call you my most intimate friends, for I reveal to you everything that I've heard from my Father."

JOHN 15:15 TPT

It's hard to imagine that Jesus thinks of us as friends. He is perfect, and we most certainly are not. He has endless patience, complete knowledge, full understanding, infinite strength, boundless energy, and everlasting love, to name a few. Us, not so much. Right? We are unequal in every possible way. We're greatly hindered by our human condition and unable to match Jesus in any way. Yet He calls us friend and withholds nothing from us.

Let that sink in. Meditate on it as you go about your day. In all your imperfection, you are loved. Your flaws do nothing to turn Him away from you. Instead, Jesus embraces your messiness and flair for drama. He sees an amazing woman He counts as a beautiful friend. Yep, what a friend you have in Jesus.

....

Father, it's hard for me to understand why You'd want to be friends with someone like me. It's not that I don't like who I am—I do. It's just that You are the Creator of everything. Sometimes Your loving-kindness just baffles me. Would You give me confidence to embrace our beautiful friendship? In Jesus' name I pray. Amen.

Look at You

Look at you, my dearest darling, you are so lovely! You are
beauty itself to me. Your passionate eyes are like gentle doves.
SONG OF SONGS 1:15 TPT

The world has been cruel to you, probably hurting your feelings more times than you can count. Maybe your childhood memories are painful. Chances are, people have put expectations on you that are wholly unrealistic, leaving you to feel like you'll never measure up. You've probably been called names or had some unflattering labels stuck to you that have made you feel ugly. Maybe some mean-spirited girls made sure you never felt accepted. Social media doesn't play fair either. Sometimes it seems like a fast track to expose your deepest insecurities because it breeds jealousy and comparison. No doubt you've been beat up, kicked around, and shut down.

But God sees your courage and resilience as beautiful. He says, *"Look at you, My strong daughter!"* He's beaming with pride that you survived, even coming out the wiser. He admires how you've refused to let the world steal your passion and purpose. And while the world may not love you for who you are, rest assured your heavenly Father delights in every part of you.

Father, thanks for seeing what it has taken to survive the ups and downs of my life. It hasn't been easy. But I know You're the reason I'm where I am today. And thank You for being proud of me. In Jesus' name I pray. Amen.

Beautiful Feet

How beautiful on the mountains are the feet of the messenger bringing good news, breaking the news that all's well, proclaiming good times, announcing salvation, telling Zion, "Your God reigns!"

ISAIAH 52:7 MSG

Wherever you go, share the good news of Jesus. Wherever your feet take you in the world, be joyful in sharing all that God has done in your life. His plan all along has been for you to shine a light on Him in the things you do and the words you speak. Maybe your mission field is in a third world country serving the poor. It could be that God has planted you in your company to proclaim His goodness to your coworkers. Maybe His plan is for you to make a difference in your community or neighborhood. And it could be that your mission is to bring the Gospel directly into your family. Regardless of where you are, your purpose is to be a messenger for God.

He looks at your feet as they take you throughout life pointing others to Him, and they are beautiful. The Lord relishes all the ways you share your testimony of His goodness. Keep walking and talking, sweet one.

....

Father, would You give me the courage and confidence to share You with people in my life? Sometimes I get scared because I'm afraid they'll judge me or reject me. Help me have the kind of faith that is bold. In Jesus' name I pray. Amen.

Hope for a Shattered Heart

He heals the wounds of every shattered heart.
PSALM 147:3 TPT

Sweet one, how has your heart been shattered? Have you faced betrayal that ripped your heart in two, making you doubt it could ever heal again? Have you been rejected because you spoke the truth to someone who didn't want to hear it? Maybe you've been abandoned by a spouse or tossed aside by someone you thought would love you forever. Has a child taken a wrong turn in life and you're scared for their safety or salvation? Maybe grief has shut you down. Or maybe you've been silenced by fear.

God makes a powerful promise to you, friend. It's not conditional. There's nothing you have to do to make it happen. You can't earn His help through good works or flowery prayers. The Lord loves you so much—sees your beautifully broken heart—and promises to heal it. Completely. Fully. Cry out to Him right now and tell Him all the ways your heart has been shattered. Surrender your brokenness. Tell God everything that has led to you being in this messy place. And then ask Him to fulfill His promise to heal.

....

Father, I am so desperate for You to restore my shattered heart.
It has been beaten and bloodied and battered by life, and I
need Your help to become whole again. I can't fix myself.
Would You please heal me? In Jesus' name I pray. Amen.

Hiding Your Beauty

As Abram was about to enter Egypt, he pulled Sarai his wife aside.
"Sarai, you are a very beautiful woman, and I am well aware that
when the Egyptians see you, they will say, 'Look, she's his wife';
then they will kill me and let you live so they can have you for them-
selves. Tell them you are my sister so that nothing will happen to
me because of you. In this way you can save my life."

GENESIS 12:11-13 VOICE

What are your thoughts about Abram's command to his wife? Was it driven by fear for him or fear for her? Do you think this was a fair request? What would you have done?

You shouldn't have to hide your beauty. It's not something to be ashamed of or something to apologize about. While you don't want to use it inappropriately to manipulate or tempt, your beauty is God-given. It's part of His intentional design. And when the Lord thought you up, He spent time deciding your personality, your appearance, the calling on your life, and every other beautiful detail of your life. So be bold and confident, always pointing to the Lord's goodness in your life.

....

Father, thank You for your intentionality in creating me. I'm sorry there
are times I complain about my body or times I use it inappropriately.
I know my beauty isn't a weapon or a deficit. Help me make confident
choices that glorify You. In Jesus' name I pray. Amen.

You Are More Than Your Beauty

"Bring Queen Vashti to my party! Tell her to put on her
royal crown and to wear her finest clothes. I want to
show off her beauty in front of my distinguished guests."
He did this because Queen Vashti was very beautiful.
ESTHER 1:11 VOICE

Think about how Queen Vashti must have felt being summoned to be a show-piece. The only reason the king wanted her to come to him was to show her off to those at his party. Can you imagine how awkward she would've felt if she'd walked into that room knowing all eyes were on her? He didn't want to talk about her compassionate heart, her gentle spirit, her intelligence, or her knack for whipping up a mean meat loaf. To him, her worth was her beauty. And that night she refused to be put on display.

God wants you to know that while you are very beautiful in His eyes, you are worth so much more than your looks. You're a multifaceted diamond shining countless gifts into the world. Others may focus on your brains, brawn, benevolence, or beauty. . .but the bottom line is that you are His beloved. And God made you with so much to offer those around you. Remember that.

Father, caring about my appearance gives me confidence,
but it's only a small part of who I am. Please help me keep that
truth in focus so I don't give outward beauty more importance
than it deserves. In Jesus' name I pray. Amen.

He Will Help and Hold

So don't be afraid. I am here, with you; don't be dismayed,
for I am your God. I will strengthen you, help you. I am here
with My right hand to make right and to hold you up.
ISAIAH 41:10 VOICE

How has your week been? Chances are you've experienced moments that birthed fear or panic, causing your heart to race. You have probably been discouraged, demoralized, and distraught a time or two. Maybe someone's words have wounded you. Maybe a relationship ended, a hope was dashed, a dream was shattered, or some bad news stole joy right out from under you. Have you felt rejected or abandoned? Are you grieving a loss? Are you struggling to make a decision that you know will be unpopular? It's been a week, eh?

The Lord has seen it all. He knows every heartbreak and frustration you've experienced. How could He not? You're His beautiful daughter and His eyes are always focused on you. His heart for you is always good. And because of His unshakable love, He promises never to leave your side—not for a second. He's committed to giving you strength and holding you steady through every tough situation. He's got you.

....

Father, I'm a mess today. I feel like life is beating me up. Help me feel
Your presence in these difficult situations. I can't get through them
if You're not here to help and hold. In Jesus' name I pray. Amen.

A Beautiful Desire

So may the words of my mouth, my meditation-thoughts,
and every movement of my heart be always pure and pleasing,
acceptable before your eyes, my only Redeemer, my Protector-God.
PSALM 19:14 TPT

The writer of today's verse is boldly declaring his desire with intense clarity, and it's a lofty desire. He's essentially vowing to make every word he speaks, every thought he meditates on, and every choice he makes something that pleases the Lord. It is a beautiful hope for living and loving with God's approval in mind. And while the goal may not be perfection (because who can attain that?), it is saturated with purpose and intentionality.

Take inventory of your life. Think about the words you speak. Are they words that would please God, or do you wince at the realization that He hears them? What about your thoughts? Do you think about things that glorify God, or do you let your mind wander down any old road? And what about your decisions and actions? Are they pure in motive and pleasing to God?

Like the psalmist, make your own declaration to the Lord today. Tell Him how you want your life to be acceptable in His eyes. And know that He will see your beautiful desire and bless you for it.

....

Father, I want my life to glorify You in every
way. Give me courage to change my ways and
thoughts. I love You! In Jesus' name I pray. Amen.

God Is a Purpose-Fulfiller

A person may have many ideas concerning God's plan for his life,
but only the designs of his purpose will succeed in the end.
PROVERBS 19:21 TPT

What plans have you made for your life? We are all full of plans and hopes and dreams. We're all working toward something. So think for a moment about the future plans you're holding on to.

Maybe it's finding the perfect spouse or deciding how many children you want. It could be a career goal or a plan to further your education. Is your big plan about building your own home so you can add your personal touch? Is it traveling the world to see new sights and experience new cultures? Maybe you want to serve God in a third world country or start a ministry in your own community. Perhaps you'd like to move to a new city, learn a new language, get into politics, or free up time to volunteer locally. Friend, what are your plans?

God created you with a mind to dream and explore new opportunities. He loves your desire to create a full and beautiful life! But unless your desires fit into His purpose for your life, they will remain dreams. He's not a hope-killer. God is a purpose-fulfiller. And you will love the future He has planned just for you.

....

Father, help me trust in the future You have designed
for me. And give me the courage and confidence
to walk it out. In Jesus' name I pray. Amen.

The Beauty of Pruning

"I am a true sprouting vine, and the farmer who tends the
vine is my Father. He cares for the branches connected to
me by lifting and propping up the fruitless branches and
pruning every fruitful branch to yield a greater harvest."

JOHN 15:1–2 TPT

No one likes the idea of being pruned. We never look forward to having the Lord clip and trim away parts of our life that aren't bearing fruit. We usually cling to those parts with all our might, or maybe we never realized there was anything to be pruned. But notice in the verse above that pruning is considered caring. God cares for you, and therefore He prunes you so that you can produce and enjoy more fruit in your life.

Ask God to show you people and places that may need to be removed. Are certain relationships or activities pulling you down? Is a mind-set or belief system causing a break in your communication with the Lord? Are your choices leading you down pathways that are dangerously close to sinful behavior? God wants you to produce a beautiful harvest with your one and only life, and He's invested in you enough to intervene when needed.

....

Father, I trust You to prune the areas of my life that need it.
Help me be willing to make changes when You show them to me.
I want to live my life in Your will. In Jesus' name I pray. Amen.

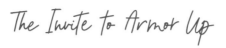

The Invite to Armor Up

Put on God's complete set of armor provided for us,
so that you will be protected as you fight against
the evil strategies of the accuser!
EPHESIANS 6:11 TPT

You were never designed to battle the things of this world alone. Being severely limited by your human condition, you need God's help to walk life out well. He knows what's coming your way and sees the pitfalls and sucker punches you'll encounter. You have a real enemy who's constantly scheming ways to discourage and dismantle your heart. But you're God's beautiful daughter with whom He is deliriously delighted; that's why He made a way for you to not only survive but thrive.

His complete set of armor is always available to you, and He invites you to put it on every day. Take some time to read Ephesians 6 to understand what His armor entails. You're a warrior, sweet one. And life can be a battle. Accept the provisions your Father has made for His beloved.

Father, sometimes I feel so ill-equipped to handle all the messes in my life.
They seem overwhelming and I get discouraged, and too often I just want
to give up and walk away. Thank You for thinking of me as You created
Your armor. Give me courage to suit up and navigate the tough times.
I know I can do anything with You. In Jesus' name I pray. Amen.

Courage to Ask

*Just ask and it will be given to you; seek after it and you will
find. Continue to knock and the door will be opened for you.
All who ask receive. Those who seek, find what they seek.
And he who knocks, will have the door opened.*

MATTHEW 7:7-8 VOICE

The Lord doesn't try to hide from you. He may be full of mystery, but God would never hide truth from you. He'd never hide Himself. Instead, God is clear when He says you'll find answers when you ask. Your prayers are heard. Every guttural cry or whispered plea reaches the heavens and finds God's ear. Every spoken and unspoken request is intimately known by Him. And while you may feel your prayers are just bouncing off the ceiling and going unanswered, that's not reality. Asking requires patience and trust, believing God will answer in the perfect timing and in the perfect way.

The Lord loves the beautiful display of courage you show when you make your needs known. He admires your faith in persevering for answers. And He promises when you seek Him, you will find Him. Keep asking.

....

*Father, I'm so glad to know You hear every request I lay
before You—even the ones that aren't beautifully articulated.
I'm glad there's no formula to follow or perfect words that need
to be said. I will keep asking and seeking and will trust Your
answers and timing. In Jesus' name I pray. Amen.*

How Does He Know?

Make God the utmost delight and pleasure of your life,
and he will provide for you what you desire the most.
PSALM 37:4 TPT

Watching a beloved daughter find delight in Him brings God great joy. Listening as she lists off the ways she's thankful for how He has impacted her life warms His heart. Hearing her share all the moments she's seen Him show up at just the right time and in just the right way means the world to God. Did you know that being excited to share a victory with the Lord or just talk about your day puts a huge smile on God's face? Making time for God blesses Him.

Think about it. Do you make God the utmost delight and pleasure of your life? How does He know how you feel about Him? How do you involve God in your everyday comings and goings? Do you connect with Him on the regular? A special assurance is attached to your finding a way to make God the center: when you choose to put Him at the top of your list of priorities, He promises to give you the desires of your beautiful heart.

....

Father, I'm sorry for not always making You the delight and pleasure
of my life. I'm sorry I've allowed other things to be prioritized above
You. I want You to reign in my life in every way. Help me find joy
in our relationship. In Jesus' name I pray. Amen.

Smile at Your Father

Look at him; give him your warmest smile.
Never hide your feelings from him.

PSALM 34:5 MSG

God wants to hear it all. He wants to know every detail of the situation, every crazy moment with that person, all the frustrations of your current circumstances, and all the emotions that come with these things. He wants to be the first one you confide in and the last one you think of when you close your eyes. God wants your heart to desire a relationship with Him because He looks at you, His beautiful daughter, and craves the same thing.

You are never too much for Him. He never thinks you're not enough. Your drama doesn't turn Him away from you, and He never thinks you're too high maintenance. You can't ruminate too much with Him, and He promises to listen every time you need to circle the mountain again. The Lord is the ultimate processor, and He never grows tired of you. You are deeply loved, fully seen, completely known.

Look up at your Father in heaven and smile. Tell Him how you feel about Him. And know that He is all ears for you.

Father, my heart is full for You too! Too often, I forget how much You love me, and I forget Your desire to be in community with me. I am committed to spending more time with You, Lord. I love You. In Jesus' name I pray. Amen.

Faithful and Trustworthy

*"The one who manages the little he has been given with
faithfulness and integrity will be promoted and trusted with
greater responsibilities. But those who cheat with the little they
have been given will not be considered trustworthy to receive more."*
LUKE 16:10 TPT

Choose to be a woman who is trustworthy. Be someone who shows faithfulness in stewarding what God has given you. Be full of integrity and do the work set before you. Love your family with great intentionality. Raise your kids to be kind. Support your husband as you grow your marriage to last. Pour time and effort into friendships. Be mindful in your career, treating others with honor and respect. Be a fantastic coworker or thoughtful boss. Embrace your neighbors, caring for the community you live in. Treat strangers with compassion. The Lord will increase your territory because of your dependability.

Choose to say yes to God's will for your life. Follow His plan to live and love others well. He will see your trustworthiness as a beautiful gift of surrender and will bless you with even more. What a privilege to partner with God's work here on earth!

....

*Father, help me be determined and diligent to walk out the
life You have planned for me. Whether in my family, with my
friends, in my career, or in other areas, I want to be full of faith
and integrity as I follow Your path. In Jesus' name I pray. Amen.*

Beautiful Strength

If your faith remains strong, even while surrounded by life's
difficulties, you will continue to experience the untold blessings
of God! True happiness comes as you pass the test with faith, and
receive the victorious crown of life promised to every lover of God!
JAMES 1:12 TPT

What are the difficult things in your life right now? Is it tension in a marriage or frustration with a child? Has an important friendship felt uncertain and you're not sure what to do next? Are finances presenting a problem, or does a scary diagnosis need to be navigated? Maybe you're facing an unexpected divorce or trying to cope with the loss of a parent, and the grief feels overwhelming. Chances are you know the feeling of being surrounded by spine-weakening and spirit-breaking circumstances that make you want to give up and walk away. But hold tightly to God, courageous one. Because it's your tenacity that will bring blessings.

When the Lord looks at you, He sees His beautifully brave daughter with a heart full of hope. He sees your resolve for restoration. God sees the steadfastness of your faith. And when you decide to stand strong through struggles and refuse to crumble in fear, He will bless you beyond belief.

....

Father, fighting the battles of this life is sapping my strength. I'm tired
from the struggles I'm facing right now. Please give me faith that holds me
up so I can pass the test and find victory. In Jesus' name I pray. Amen.

The Call To Love

Now, this is the goal: to live in harmony with one another and demonstrate affectionate love, sympathy, and kindness toward other believers. Let humility describe who you are as you dearly love one another. Never retaliate when someone treats you wrongly, nor insult those who insult you, but instead, respond by speaking a blessing over them—because a blessing is what God promised to give you.

1 PETER 3:8-9 TPT

To God, a loving heart is a beautiful heart. His goal—His hope—is for us to be an encouragement to those around us. God wants us to show our care through our actions. His plan is that we become an extension of Jesus, showing sympathy and kindness whenever possible. The Lord esteems humility; it's a characteristic He finds especially delightful. Loving with a humble heart, choosing not to be easily offended or to plot revenge, shows God how you've matured in your faith. And embracing the call to treat others with care reveals the beauty of your heart and spirit.

It may feel like a tall order, but choosing to live with such intentionality will bring blessing upon blessing into your life.

....

Father, the truth is that sometimes I don't want to love others. I don't want to show compassion and kindness because I've been hurt. Would You give me a heart that longs to please You in this way? I need Your help to love the people You've placed in my life. In Jesus' name I pray. Amen.

Who Are Your Role Models?

The prophets who declared the word of the Lord are your role models, my brothers and sisters, for what it means to live patiently in the face of suffering. Look, we bless and honor the memory of those who persevered under hardship. Remember how Job endured and how the Lord orchestrated the triumph of his final circumstances as a grand display of His mercy and compassion.

JAMES 5:10–11 VOICE

The world gives us countless role models to fashion our lives after. Some are made out to be modern-day gods, idols we place above everyone else. We're told to talk like them, act like them, and dress like them. But the problem is that we're following the wrong people.

God wants us to look to those who have lived with hope while facing tremendous hardships, seeing how they waited patiently for His plan to unfold. He tells us to try to live up to the example of those who stood courageously and didn't give up even when they felt heartbroken by their situation.

You'll find this kind of role model in the Bible, where many amazing men and women have set a beautiful example for us. But also take a minute to think about the people you know who have lived this way. When you're wise about whom you choose to admire, your discernment pleases God.

....

Father, help me find role models who glorify You with their lives. In Jesus' name I pray. Amen.

Beautifully Unblemished

*Now to Him who is able to keep you from stumbling or falling into sin,
and to present you unblemished [blameless and faultless] in the presence
of His glory with triumphant joy and unspeakable delight, to the only God
our Savior, through Jesus Christ our Lord, be glory, majesty, dominion,
and power, before all time and now and forever. Amen.*

JUDE 1:24–25 AMP

We all have blemishes the world finds ugly. It may be something physical that doesn't quite fit into what others say is beautiful; we may not meet the world's standards of attractiveness. But those blemishes could also be marks on our life that are used against us, like a scarlet letter of sorts. What are yours? Maybe you've been labeled as a divorcee, an adulterer, a single mom, or an old maid. Maybe you've had some trouble with the law, got fired from a job, or didn't finish high school. To the world, these blemishes can mark us as undesirable, unwanted.

But keep your chin up, sweet one. To God, you're beautifully unblemished. All of those things others may use to judge you mean nothing to *the* Judge. You are His daughter with whom He is well pleased. No one else's opinion matters.

....

*Father, I'm so grateful You see me for who I really am
and that I'm pleasing in Your sight! Help me ignore the
judgments of others. In Jesus' name I pray. Amen.*

Trusting No Matter What

*So Joshua went up from Gilgal, he and all the warriors
with him and all the mighty men of valor. And the Lord
said to Joshua, Do not fear them, for I have given them into
your hand; there shall not a man of them stand before you.*

JOSHUA 10:7–8 AMPC

Sometimes you stand in battle not knowing the outcome or the timing or God's plan for the tough season you're trying to navigate. While your faith may be activated, you're still choosing to trust God without knowing the way things will turn out. Other times God is very clear, telling you victory will be yours. You may still have to walk out the situation with integrity and intentionality, but you're promised that you will come out the other side successful.

Regardless, God desires your trust. Whether you need to exercise blind faith or you have a confident faith, He wants you to know that His heart for you is good. Deciding to trust God is a beautiful example of your maturity, and the Lord delights to see that depth of belief in His beloved daughter. Remember that He is always with you. He is always for you. And you are loved.

*Father, I don't need to have answers to trust You. My faith is strong
enough to know that You've got me no matter what. All I need to
do is believe and follow Your lead. In Jesus' name I pray. Amen.*

He Cares What You Wear

*Since you are all set apart by God, made holy and
dearly loved, clothe yourselves with a holy way of life:
compassion, kindness, humility, gentleness, and patience.*
COLOSSIANS 3:12 VOICE

It matters to God what you choose to wear. It's not that He has an opinion on whether you should wear a turtleneck or a tank top, leggings or capris, a skirt or shorts, flats or heels. What He cares about most is what you wear on the inside, because those are the things affecting your life on the outside.

The Lord sees your beauty shining through when you live an intentional life that glorifies Him. When you show compassion to a stranger on the street or choose to be kind to someone who is mean for sport, He is impressed. In those moments you want to toot your own horn and boast about yourself but decide to stay humble instead, God is moved. When you are gentle and patient with your family and friends when it would be easier to unleash frustration, the Lord is pleased.

Be the kind of woman who chooses God's wardrobe over the offerings of the world. Being a blessing to others is beautiful.

....

*Father, I want to clothe myself in the things that matter most
to You because they help me live my best life. Help me be
intentional to wear compassion, kindness, humility, gentleness,
and patience every day. In Jesus' name I pray. Amen.*

Glorifying God with Your Work

Put your heart and soul into every activity you do, as though
you are doing it for the Lord himself and not merely for others.
For we know that we will receive a reward, an inheritance from
the Lord, as we serve the Lord Yahweh, the Anointed One!
COLOSSIANS 3:23–24 TPT

The Lord loves to see you acting with care and integrity in the things you do. To watch His daughter pour her talents into worthwhile projects and her time into community-building is so pleasing to Him. He appreciates your willingness to sacrifice for the kingdom. And when you do, God wants you to know it's like working directly for the Lord Himself.

Where are you doing this well? Where are you working with intentionality, staying focused in a tough situation because you know God has put you here for this season? Where are you making a difference? Where could you be doing this better? In what activities do you need to refocus, remembering who is glorified in a job well done?

....

Father, I confess that I sometimes give less than my best at work
and at home. I may be tired or frustrated, but those aren't excuses.
I'm sorry for not recognizing that You expect me to work on earth to
glorify You in heaven. I am committed to changing my attitude. And
thanks for loving me even when I mess up. In Jesus' name I pray. Amen.

Unbreakable Promises

Still, the Lord is true to His promises; He will hold
you up and guard you against the evil one.

2 THESSALONIANS 3:3 VOICE

In a world full of failed promises, it's good to remember that the Lord always keeps His promises. Always. He is a constant in a world of inconsistency. He won't flake out on you, leaving you without help or hope. Instead, you can fully trust that if God has made a promise to you, it will come to pass. His pledge is unbreakable. Unshakable. And never once has He failed to do what He has said He will do. The Lord is true to His promises.

That means you can trust that He will be there to protect you. God will give you wisdom and discernment when you need them. He will restore those things that have been taken from you—the things stolen by hard seasons of life. He will be available whenever you need Him, day or night. He won't walk away from you or ignore your pleas for His intervention. Why? Because you are God's beautiful daughter, and His heart for you is always good. Even in your mess, you're a delight to Him.

....

Father, help me in my times of trouble. Hold me up when I am weak and
scared. Remind me of who I am and who You are. And help me remember
that Your promises are unbreakable. In Jesus' name I pray. Amen.

Don't Be Afraid to Step Out

For God will never give you the spirit of fear, but the
Holy Spirit who gives you mighty power, love, and self-control.
2 TIMOTHY 1:7 TPT

Fear is a nasty emotion that can often paralyze us from taking the next right step God has planned. We worry we won't be able to do what we need to, or that we won't be able to do it well enough. We're concerned we may not be hearing God correctly, and that shakes our confidence to follow His lead. We're scared we'll bite off more than we can chew and feel overwhelmed because it will require too much of us. We worry others will find us silly, and we'll end up embarrassed. Fear is a big deal that causes big anxiety. But it's not from God.

Sweet one, you were created with mighty power. You were made from love and for loving others well. You have the unique ability to show self-control at any moment and in every situation. Fear isn't in your DNA. God made you beautifully bold, able to do amazing things with confidence and courage. So when you feel fear rising up, tell it to leave. And then remind yourself of all the good things God has put inside you.

....

Father, I confess that fear is something I struggle with. But
knowing it's not from You gives me the strength to command
it to leave. Help me be unafraid! In Jesus' name I pray. Amen.

The Ugly Critical Spirit

"Refuse to be a critic full of bias toward others, and judgment will not be passed on you. For you'll be judged by the same standard that you've used to judge others. The measurement you use on them will be used on you. Why would you focus on the flaw in someone else's life and yet fail to notice the glaring flaws of your own?"

MATTHEW 7:1–3 TPT

Take a personal inventory. Who are you judging for the way they look or the way they act? Who are you belittling, even if you're not doing it in front of friends or family? Where is your critical spirit in overdrive? Are you being a hater of a group of people or those who believe a certain way?

A critical spirit is ugly. The practice of tearing down others is a dangerous path to be walking on, because it not only hurts people but also displeases God. He's asking us to refuse to sit in the judgment seat. Even more, the ways you criticize others are the same ways you'll be criticized. The measuring stick you use will be turned on you. The ways you condemn others will be the ways you're condemned. This is a weighty warning.

Be the kind of woman who lets God be judge and jury and chooses instead to be full of love and grace. Because it's that mind-set He calls beautiful.

....

Father, help me affirm the good in others rather than be critical. In Jesus' name I pray. Amen.

143

The Beauty of Confidence

"Be strong. Take courage. Don't be intimidated. Don't give them a second thought because GOD, your God, is striding ahead of you. He's right there with you. He won't let you down; he won't leave you."
DEUTERONOMY 31:6 MSG

How would your life look different if you stood with confidence when life's storms hit, knowing God was with you and He would protect and guide you? What if you let bad news slide off of you rather than stick? What if a scary diagnosis didn't cause you to crumble in fear? What if mounting bills didn't make you hide under the covers? There's no question this confident approach to life would take epic faith to walk out, but what if?

Sweet one, God loves a woman full of faith. He delights in a daughter who chooses to trust that He is in control and believes He won't let her down or leave her to fend for herself. The Lord finds that kind of confidence in Him beautiful.

....

Father, I confess that I freak out sometimes. It's hard to look at my circumstances and not let fear creep in. Choosing to trust You isn't always easy. It's not always my first stop. Would You give me the grit to keep my eyes on You rather than drowning in the difficulties that come my way? I need Your help to keep my confidence anchored in You every day. In Jesus' name I pray. Amen.

A Heart Full of Faith

The Lord is my Strength and my Song, and He has become my
Salvation; this is my God, and I will praise Him, my father's God,
and I will exalt Him. The Lord is a Man of War; the Lord is His name.

EXODUS 15:2–3 AMPC

Today's verse is part of the song that Moses and the Israelites sang to God after the Red Sea miracle that saved them from Pharaoh's army after they walked out of Egypt. It was a moment of praise for the radical deliverance they just witnessed. They literally had a sea in front of them and an army behind them, and God made a way out. He answered their cries for help. They knew that unless God showed up, they were going to die. They had no other option but to trust Him.

A heart full of faith pleases the Lord. He delights in the belief of His people because He knows how difficult it can be to trust an unknown future to a God we can't see or touch. Where do you need to trust that He will make a way out of the tough circumstances you're facing? Where do you need to surrender your fears and stand in faith? Do it, friend. If you're going to err, err on the side of faith. It's that choice God sees as a beautiful one.

....

Father, I trust You. In Jesus' name I pray. Amen.

And She Believed God

And he [Abram] believed in (trusted in, relied on,
remained steadfast to) the Lord, and He counted
it to him as righteousness (right standing with God).
GENESIS 15:6 AMPC

It takes a lot of grit to believe God over the challenging circumstances we'll face in life. It's not always an easy choice to make, especially when it seems the light at the end of the tunnel is a freight train barreling toward us. Too often we let our fears get the best of us and assume the worst outcomes and endings. But giving in to fear paralyzes us from living our best life. It keeps us from activating our faith.

What if, instead, you chose to believe God's promises—the ones He whispers to you and the ones He shares in His Word? It may take all you have to refuse to give up and instead wait on the Lord to straighten out the crooked path. But to God, steadfastness is a beautiful decision, and He counts it as righteousness. Friend, this kind of faith is what makes you right with God.

. . . .

Father, I don't always understand the why, but I'm choosing to trust
the Who. This isn't a natural choice for me because I look at all
the negatives and then fear creeps in. Please increase my faith so I
can trust in You and not give in to what's scaring me. I need Your
confidence and courage right now. In Jesus' name I pray. Amen.

A Worthwhile Investment

*What I'm getting at, friends, is that you should simply keep on doing
what you've done from the beginning. When I was living among
you, you lived in responsive obedience. Now that I'm separated
from you, keep it up. Better yet, redouble your efforts. Be energetic
in your life of salvation, reverent and sensitive before God. That
energy is God's energy, an energy deep within you, God himself
willing and working at what will give him the most pleasure.*

PHILIPPIANS 2:12-13 MSG

Every day, God is working in you. It may not feel that way, especially on those days when you're particularly cranky and wretched toward others. But not even your ornery behavior can change the truth of His plan for your life. God didn't only create you; He also chooses to invest in you. And whether you realize it or not, He's intentionally working in your heart to help you want to do the things that glorify Him and to live in a way that pleases Him. And even more, the Lord gives you the power to do it! What a relief to know we don't have to walk out His divine plan in our dinky human strength.

Your Father thinks of everything, doesn't He? And when He looks at you—His beautiful daughter—He knows His investment is well worth His time.

....

*Father, You really do think of everything. Thank You for finding me
worthy of Your time, effort, and care. In Jesus' name I pray. Amen.*

A Seat at the Table

*He raised us up with Him and seated us in the heavenly realms
with our beloved Jesus the Anointed, the Liberating King. He did
this for a reason: so that for all eternity we will stand as a living
testimony to the incredible riches of His grace and kindness that
He freely gives to us by uniting us with Jesus the Anointed.*
EPHESIANS 2:6–7 VOICE

It's hard to imagine that one day, if we've chosen to accept Jesus as our Savior, we will sit with Him in heaven. When we look at our bad attitude or rude comments, our critical spirit or self-righteous stance, our selfish ways or seasons of sinning, the idea of taking a seat next to Christ seems outlandish. But His ways of thinking aren't ours, and His will is far superior to the will we exert. The truth is that God adores you. He's crazy about you even though you're flawed and feisty. Your snarky ways and stinky whims don't deter His love. He sees deeper, knowing your beauty inside and out. And it's because of His desire to bless you for eternity that God gives you a seat at the table with His Son.

Take time to thank Him for all the ways He blesses you. Show your gratitude for His compassion.

. . . .

*Father, help me acknowledge Your grace and kindness
every day. I love You. In Jesus' name I pray. Amen.*

Beauty from the Ashes

Even though you intended to harm me, God intended
it only for good, and through me, He preserved the
lives of countless people, as He is still doing today.
GENESIS 50:20 VOICE

This concept is so very powerful, friend. It's lofty and weighty. It's hearty like meat and potatoes. And if you can grab onto this truth, it will change how you view your circumstances. It will help you breathe and give you courage to take a step back from a complete meltdown. Yes, it takes grit to trust that God works out everything for good, and it takes faith in epic proportions to walk out this belief, but deciding to look at your struggles through this filter will give you hope and a fresh perspective.

So when your friend abandons you, husband betrays you, child rejects you, boss fires you, or acquaintance harshly criticizes you, remember those harmful things will work toward your benefit. You may not see it immediately or it may not happen the way you hoped, but the Lord only allows hardship into your life with the purpose of using it to make you shine brighter. He promises to make beauty from ashes every time.

....

Father, help me trust that You will restore me when I get knocked down.
Give me an eternal perspective so I can trust that You see me and
will help me, and bless me with a steadfast hope that You'll make
everything good in the end. In Jesus' name I pray. Amen.

You're an Original

So may we never be arrogant, or look down on another,
for each of us is an original. We must forsake all jealousy
that diminishes the value of others.

GALATIANS 5:26 TPT

Can we be honest? Sometimes we're the ones to feel judged, but all too often we're the ones who feel superior to those around us. We are critical, even if our criticism remains unspoken. If we make more money, we may feel overly proud of ourselves. Or we may be arrogant because our kid is the best player on the team, our husband is more attentive, our home is larger, our vacations are more lavish, and so on. We may even feel loftier than our divorced neighbor or the homeless man we pass on the street. But God wants us to have compassion for one another, not condemnation.

Everyone is an original creation. The Lord made each of us with great intentionality, careful to think through the details of our person. When we decide we're better than another, we're essentially criticizing God. We're judging His work, telling Him it's lacking.

When you choose to see everyone as an original masterpiece, you are honoring God. You are respecting the Lord's handiwork. We all have value, and each one of us is beautiful in God's eyes.

....

Father, help me see others through Your eyes. Give me a heart
of compassion. Let me be willing to appreciate differences
rather than sit in judgment. In Jesus' name I pray. Amen.

Beautifully Exposed

*As a result of this encounter, Hagar decided to give the Eternal
One who had spoken to her a special name because He had seen
her in her misery. "I'm going to call You the God of Seeing because
in this place I have seen the One who watches over me."*

GENESIS 16:13 VOICE

When you feel unnoticed, let today's verse encourage your heart. Others may not see the pain in your eyes, but God does. Others may not be aware of the fear that's paralyzing you, but the Lord is completely aware. Your responses may be misunderstood, but He knows exactly what's behind them. Maybe you hide your insecurities from those around you, but they are fully known to God. Friend, He sees you. He understands you. He watches over you. And absolutely nothing going on in your life—no emotion, feeling, or thought—is hidden from the One who created you.

The world encourages you to grin and bear it. They tell you to let it go and move on. Their advice is to fake it till you make it. And you may feel shame because of your brokenness. But the depths of your heart are beautifully exposed to God, and He promises to heal the broken places for you. Let Him.

....

*Father, thank You for seeing me clearly and without judgment.
Please heal my heart from this overwhelming pain. I can't
do it on my own. In Jesus' name I pray. Amen.*

Beautiful Perseverance

I will continue to rejoice because I know that through your encouragement and prayers and through the help of the Spirit of Jesus the Anointed, I will soon be released from this dark place.
PHILIPPIANS 1:18-19 VOICE

It takes guts and grit to continue choosing joy when you'd rather curl up in bed with ice cream and Netflix. It's not easy to be happy when your world seems to be crumbling around you. Enduring life's struggles isn't easy. But when you decide to persevere through the dark times, trusting that God is working things out for your good, you are showing the world what faith looks like. You are modeling for others that you can still have a good life even when it's hard. And that impresses the Lord.

Your perseverance is beautiful to Him because He understands how difficult it is to be steadfast. He knows the burden of long-suffering. So your deliberate decision to continue rejoicing and waiting on His intervention pleases God. It moves Him. And it's that kind of radical trust that will significantly establish your faith.

....

Father, sometimes perseverance feels almost impossible, especially when I'm losing hope that everything will be okay. Would You please give me the confidence and courage to make this tough choice? Give me a supportive community and constant reminders that You're with me. And please deliver me from this dark place. In Jesus' name I pray. Amen.

True to His Word

*God is not a man—He doesn't lie. God isn't the son of a man
to want to take back what He's said, or say something
and not follow through, or speak and not act on it.*
NUMBERS 23:19 VOICE

What a great reminder that God is a God of His word. Unlike others, He doesn't lie. He's incapable of it. God is a truth-teller through and through, and that's why we can believe unwaveringly that He is who He says He is and that we are who He says we are. Once He speaks, it can't be undone. The Lord won't go back on His Word. And even more, when God says He is going to do something, it will be done. He'll always follow through.

That's a powerful truth to hold on to. Think about it. What has He promised you? Is there a certain promise from the Bible that you're clinging to, feeling confident that it's a promise for you too? Maybe you're holding tight to God's promise to restore a relationship or open a door for a new job. Or His promise to return a wayward child or heal an ailment. Or maybe His promise to give you a sense of peace and comfort as you navigate a tough season in life. Choosing to believe God is a beautiful display of faith. And He sees it.

*Father, thank You for being truthful and trustworthy.
I'm choosing to place my faith in Your promises!
In Jesus' name I pray. Amen.*

153

This Is Who You Are

For you are a holy and set-apart people to the Lord your God;
the Lord your God has chosen you to be a special people to
Himself out of all the peoples on the face of the earth.
DEUTERONOMY 7:6 AMPC

Sweet one, who do others say you are? A disgrace? High maintenance? Unlovable? Overemotional? Ugly? Stupid? We all have critics who are quick to label us with untruths. While they may think these hurtful sticky notes are accurate, the Lord does not. Not at all. Instead, He thinks the world of you. Every day, you delight His heart. And His opinion of who you are always trumps the opinions of others.

Never mind the haters; here's who you are in God's eyes: He made you holy, setting you apart when you accepted Jesus as your Savior. You're chosen, and you always will be. That cannot be undone. God wants you. He picked you. And, friend, you're special in every way. You are a beautiful addition to the family of God. So when the world shouts horrible things about you, listen instead for God's whisper of truth.

Father, thank You for telling me who I am so I don't have to believe the hurtful labels from the world. You are a good God, and I'm so thankful You've made me holy, chosen, and special. In Jesus' name I pray. Amen.

Because God Loves You

Therefore, know in your heart (be fully cognizant) that the LORD your God disciplines and instructs you just as a man disciplines and instructs his son. Therefore, you shall keep the commandments of the LORD your God, to walk [that is, to live each and every day] in His ways and fear [and worship] Him [with awe-filled reverence and profound respect].

DEUTERONOMY 8:5–6 AMP

I think if we're honest, we admit we deeply dislike discipline. We don't like when we suffer the natural consequences of our sin, and it's difficult to admit we've messed up and could do better. We may rebel against constructive criticism, not finding it to be constructive at all. And having others point out our shortcomings doesn't leave us with a warm and fuzzy feeling. At the core, the truth is that we'd rather not be corrected by anyone for our actions.

But God disciplines and instructs you because He loves you. His way of living is the best way, and because He wants the best for you, the Lord will correct your course. Choosing to receive and embrace His instruction is a beautiful response and shows a maturity of faith!

Father, I'll admit I don't like when others correct me. Maybe it's that rebellious streak in me. But I trust that You only discipline because You want the best for me. Help me welcome it. In Jesus' name I pray. Amen.

Completely and Wonderfully Free

*Let me be clear, the Anointed One has set us free—not partially,
but completely and wonderfully free! We must always cherish this
truth and stubbornly refuse to go back into the bondage of our past.*

GALATIANS 5:1 TPT

When humanity adopted a sinful nature, creating a chasm between us and God, He made a way to make things right. The Lord asked Jesus to step off His throne, put on skin, and step into the world with one purpose in mind—to free us from our sin. Not partially free, but completely and wonderfully free.

It's tricky, you know. Sin has a way of binding you up and holding you hostage. Before you realize it, your joy is lost. Your confidence is compromised. And your peace is hijacked. Sin separates you from God and keeps you from living a holy and righteous life. Because of His love for you, God couldn't let you stay separated, so He sent His perfect Son to save you, His beautiful daughter. The result was your freedom—freedom to love and live with purpose. Hold on to that hard-won liberation every day!

. . . .

*Father, I'm so thankful for what Jesus did on the cross for me. I'm thankful
You loved me enough to ask Him for such a powerful sacrifice. Help me
choose to hold on to that freedom rather than return to the bondage of
my past. I don't want that any longer! In Jesus' name I pray. Amen.*

The Holy Spirit's Job

After this, the church all over Judea, Galilee, and Samaria experienced
a season of peace. The congregations grew larger and larger, with the
believers being empowered and encouraged by the Holy Spirit. They
worshiped God in wonder and awe, and walked in the fear of the Lord.

ACTS 9:31 TPT

The Holy Spirit is God living in you—His deposit of goodness that helps you live out the calling on your life. The Holy Spirit gives you that gut feeling warning you of bad choices ahead. The Holy Spirit helps you understand the Bible and discern what God wants you to know. The Spirit leads you into worship and repentance. And because God cares for His children, when you say yes to Jesus, the Spirit comes alive in your heart. What a beautiful expression of His love!

Thank God today for His incredible gift of empowerment and encouragement. Tell Him about times you've felt the nudge, the discernment, the warning, and the desire to praise. Tell God why His Holy Spirit makes a difference in your life. And share with Him ways your life is more beautiful because He is a part of it.

....

Father, You think of everything. What a brilliant idea to leave Your
Spirit here—in our hearts—to be a powerful force as we walk out our
faith. You knew we'd need help to live with intentionality and gave us
exactly what we needed. I love You. In Jesus' name I pray. Amen.

The Benefits of Being His Daughter

*And so that we would know for sure that we are his true children,
God released the Spirit of Sonship into our hearts—moving us to cry
out intimately, "My Father! You're our true Father!" Now we're no longer
living like slaves under the law, but we enjoy being God's very own
sons and daughters! And because we're his, we can access everything
our Father has—for we are heirs of God through Jesus, the Messiah!*

GALATIANS 4:6-7 TPT

Have you ever considered—like really thought through—the truth that you're a child of God? He chose you to be His beautiful daughter. It's a pretty hefty realization, and it's one we struggle to embrace because we often feel unworthy of such a title. We wonder how a perfect God could love such an imperfect woman. We think it's just a matter of time before we cross His proverbial line in the sand for the last time and He walks away. We worry that our flawed actions or thoughts will disqualify us, or our sinful nature will ruin His adoration. But none of that is true.

Not only will God call you daughter for eternity, but He also promises access to Him. You can confidently ask for anything the Father has—strength, perspective, hope, provision, wisdom, love—and it will be given to you!

....

*Father, what a privilege to be Your daughter!
In Jesus' name I pray. Amen.*

The Look of Love

Look at how much encouragement you've found in your relationship
with the Anointed One! You are filled to overflowing with his comforting
love. You have experienced a deepening friendship with the Holy Spirit
and have felt his tender affection and mercy.

PHILIPPIANS 2:1 TPT

God looks at you and sees His beautiful daughter. He sees fresh determination on your face and a strong resolve in your heart. He is delighted by your gusto for a relationship with Him because He knows how it fills your love bucket and gives you renewed energy for the day. He sees all the ways you're trying to go deeper with Him, making time and space for God in your everyday life. The Lord loves that you've chosen to share your struggles through tears and your victories through giggles and gratitude. That kind of intentionality is always rewarded!

Make no mistake that a woman steeped in time with the Lord has the look of love. It manifests in strength, determination, peace, freedom, joy, and surrender. And, sweet one, it's a beautiful look on you.

....

Father, thanks for reminding me how time with You changes everything.
Life is hard and messy, and I need the kind of encouragement that
brings lasting fulfillment. I crave Your comforting love and kindness as
I walk out the struggles before me. And I am so thankful to experience
Your affection and mercy every day. In Jesus' name I pray. Amen.

The Beauty of Unity

So I'm asking you, my friends, that you be joined together in perfect unity—with one heart, one passion, and united in one love. Walk together with one harmonious purpose and you will fill my heart with unbounded joy.
PHILIPPIANS 2:2 TPT

The apostle Paul knew the value of community, and he understood how powerful a unified community could be. When people are working together for a common purpose, a beautiful synergy emerges, fostering creativity and empowerment. Maybe you've experienced this kind of synergy in times of worship or moments of corporate prayer. It can happen when you work with others on a mission field, support a friend who is recovering from surgery, help a widow navigate a new normal, or come together with others for a fund-raising event. When like-minded people work in harmony, great things can happen!

Ask the Lord to make unity with others a desire of your heart. Be willing to join in with others to further a cause. Find time to connect with community in meaningful ways. Be intentional to find friends who share your desire to work toward a common goal. The result will be beautiful.

....

Father, give me a heart to pursue unity with others. Cultivate in me a desire to find community and walk with others in harmonious purpose. I understand the value it offers to me as well as the way it pleases Your heart! In Jesus' name I pray. Amen.

Breathing Room

*But me he caught—reached all the way from sky to sea; he pulled me out
of that ocean of hate, that enemy chaos, the void in which I was drowning.
They hit me when I was down, but GOD stuck by me. He stood me up on
a wide-open field; I stood there saved—surprised to be loved!*

PSALM 18:16-19 MSG

Do you remember a time when you felt the walls closing in on you? You felt
suffocated by your situation, unable to catch your breath before the next wave
hit. You had no safe place to hide and felt vulnerable and exposed. Can you
think back to a time when enemies seemed to surround you on all sides, and
you weren't sure who you could trust? No doubt we've all had seasons like
that. Life is hard. And no one gets through it without feeling overwhelmed by
their circumstances.

Let this passage of scripture encourage your heart. It's the perfect reminder
that you are seen by God and that He knows just what you need right when you
need it. The Lord loves you and promises never to leave you. He will rescue
His beautiful beloved and give you the breathing room you need to thrive.

....

*Father, I need You to rescue me from enemy chaos.
Please pull me out of it and set me in a wide-open field
so I can catch my breath. In Jesus' name I pray. Amen.*

Glorify His Name

*For you are my high fortress, where I'm kept safe. You are to me a
stronghold of salvation. When you deliver me out of this peril, it will
bring glory to your name. As you guide me forth I'll be kept safe
from the hidden snares of the enemy—the secret traps that lie
before me—for you have become my rock of strength.*

PSALM 31:3-4 TPT

Notice the third sentence of today's passage starts with the word *when*. What a powerful reminder that God promises to deliver you from the struggles you face. It's not a matter of *if*; it's a promise of *when*. And His intervention not only helps you find freedom from oppression but also provides an opportunity for you to point others to God. It's a chance for His name to be glorified as Savior, Redeemer, Restorer, Healer, Provider, and Deliverer. And when you give God credit for the ways He has shown up in your life, He sees it as a beautiful gift from His beloved.

How has He been your high fortress, stronghold, guide, and rock of strength? Be quick to point out God's help to others, because it will encourage them that He'll also be those things in their own situation.

....

*Father, I'm sorry I don't always acknowledge how You've intervened
in my circumstances. I'm going to give You the glory so others will
be encouraged as they wait for relief. Thank You for loving
me so well. In Jesus' name I pray. Amen.*

Never Neglected

*All who are oppressed may come to you as a shelter in the time of trouble,
a perfect hiding place. May everyone who knows your mercy keep putting
their trust in you, for they can count on you for help no matter what.
O Lord, you will never, no never, neglect those who come to you.*

PSALM 9:9-10 TPT

No one likes to feel neglected. It hurts to be overlooked in a time of need or underappreciated by those around us. Being abandoned in our messiness leaves us feeling like an inconvenience, and being ignored in our heartbreak makes us feel unloved. When we're in a hard season of life, what we really need are people to come alongside us in support. Too often we feel forgotten or deserted and left to handle everything on our own. But God loves you too much to ever walk away from your troubled heart.

The Lord isn't overwhelmed or bothered by your emotions. They're never too much for Him. God sees you as His beautiful daughter, and His heart for you is always good. He invites you into His loving arms so He can shelter you in times of trouble. Trust Him with every discouragement and disappointment. You can always count on God to help!

....

*Father, the truth is that people let me down because they don't
give me what I need when I'm struggling. Help me remember to
take my worries to You instead. In Jesus' name I pray. Amen.*

Choose to Live Pure

Listen: to those who are pure, all things are pure. But to those who are tainted, stained, and unbelieving, nothing is pure because their minds and their consciences are polluted. They claim, "I know God," but their actions are a slap to His face. They are wretched, disobedient, and useless to any worthwhile cause.

TITUS 1:15–16 VOICE

God views those who are pure of heart as beautiful. It's not about being perfect, it's about living with purpose. It's choosing to show up with perseverance. It's trusting God rather than controlling or manipulating everyone around you. It's deciding to follow the right way even when it's the hard way. It's obeying God when doing what He asks is miles out of your comfort zone. It's saying yes and trusting scared.

Be mindful of the life you're living, making sure it aligns with God's best for you. Listen for His voice and direction, and be careful that you're speaking truth with love and not condemnation. Be fully aware of your actions and words, choosing to glorify God through them. He delights in His daughters when they choose to live pure.

....

Father, help me live a life of faith rather than give in to the world's polluted ways. Give me courage to choose the right things even when they're the hard things. I know I need Your help to stay on the right path. In Jesus' name I pray. Amen.

The Golden Rule

"In everything you do, be careful to treat others in the same way you'd want them to treat you, for that is the essence of all the teachings of the Law and the Prophets."

MATTHEW 7:12 TPT

This verse is known as the Golden Rule for living. It's a call to live mindfully because you reap what you sow. It's not a formula to follow. It's not a magical equation for getting what you want. You can't manipulate others with this intentionality. But rather it's a reminder to be kind and caring. It's an opportunity to think about how you're treating those around you.

Let's take inventory. How are you treating your friends? What about your family members? Are you patient and kind? Are you loving and thoughtful? Or do you take them for granted and put unrealistic expectations on them? What about strangers, like restaurant workers or store clerks? How do you treat them? Are you dismissive? Do you bark orders at them? When God sees you choosing to live and love with compassion and kindness, He delights in you! And He will bless you for it.

Father, help me embrace the concept of reaping and sowing. I want to be a positive presence in the world rather than someone who brings others down. Would You give me the strength to live this way? In Jesus' name I pray. Amen.

Alive and Active

For we have the living Word of God, which is full of energy, and it pierces more sharply than a two-edged sword. It will even penetrate to the very core of our being where soul and spirit, bone and marrow meet! It interprets and reveals the true thoughts and secret motives of our hearts.

HEBREWS 4:12 TPT

It's because God loves you so greatly and desires for you to know Him deeply that He created His Word to be alive and active even today! It's your guide for living and loving with intention. It's how to know what is right and wrong. The Bible invigorates you with passion and purpose because your soul connects to the truth.

Are you seeking guidance in a tricky situation today? What relationships are you trying to navigate that have you stumped about the next right step? Are you wondering if your choices are aligning with God's best for you? Take time to dig into His Word, because you will find what you're looking for.

....

Father, I'm so grateful You created Your Word for us. This handbook for living is such a thoughtful and tangible expression of Your love. Help me remember that You will meet me in its pages and show me the right way to go. I don't need to figure everything out on my own. In Jesus' name I pray. Amen.

Shining from the Inside Out

*"Rise up in splendor and be radiant, for your light has dawned,
and Yahweh's glory now streams from you! Look carefully! Darkness
blankets the earth, and thick gloom covers the nations, but Yahweh
arises upon you and the brightness of his glory appears over you!"*

ISAIAH 60:1–2 TPT

When you spend time with the Lord, it's evident. That kind of investment is undeniable. Your face may not be physically illuminated, but your beautiful soul will shine from the inside out. It will radiate His glory. Through the words you speak and the things you do, others will see His love, joy, peace, patience, strength, wisdom, hope, and compassion in your life. They will be unmistakable.

Keep in mind that everyone is in a battle of some sort. From relationship stressors to financial burdens to career challenges to personal struggles, we are all dealing with hardships and heartbreaks. So when you are intentional to spend time with Jesus, it's a blessing to the world. You're bringing a little slice of heaven to those who need it most. And that delights the heart of God more than you know.

....

*Father, I can feel the difference when I spend time with You.
When I'm in Your Word, I'm better equipped to love on those
around me. I am more compassionate and caring. And I hold an
eternal perspective in a tough world. Thank You for blessing me
in these ways! In Jesus' name I pray. Amen.*

167

Go Ahead and Give Thanks

Go ahead and give God thanks for all the glorious things he has done!
Go ahead and worship him! Tell everyone about his wonders! Let's
sing his praises! Sing, and put all of his miracles to music!
PSALM 105:1–2 TPT

Sometimes we squash our feelings of thanksgiving. Rather than celebrate a victory, we move on to the next thing on the to-do list. We stay focused on doing what's next instead of recognizing God's provision or restoration. We don't take the time to sit in awe of how He just showed up and saved the day. And we forget to reflect on all the ways God has been a force in our circumstances.

Let this be a reminder to take a moment to show gratitude for the Lord's presence in your life. Go ahead and give Him the praise He is worthy of! Tell Him how His kindness matters and how His timing was perfect. Your appreciativeness is beautiful to the Lord, and your worship is breathtaking. So go ahead and give thanks.

. . . .

Father, I'm sorry I don't always show You my gratitude. I'm sorry I
sometimes forget to thank You for all You do in my life. Help me see
all the ways You bless me, and give me the capacity to know You
better and appreciate You more! In Jesus' name I pray. Amen.

Letting God Shine Through You

Choose to be the kind of woman who gives glory to the Lord rather than taking credit for yourself. It wasn't karma or luck. The planets didn't have to align perfectly. Instead, be quick to let others know how God showed up in your tough situation, or how He restored a relationship you thought was lost. Of course, you had a part to play. You had to choose to participate in His great plan. But don't forget to point others to God in heaven by acknowledging the important role He played in the circumstances you've faced.

Letting God shine through you is beautiful. God loves to see you, His beloved daughter, recognizing His hand in your life. And it also puts the spotlight on His goodness, His strength, His redemption, His care, His wisdom, and the countless ways He takes care of those He loves, encouraging others to put their faith in Him.

....

Father, You deserve all the glory! Use me to reveal Your majesty!
Let my life reflect Your goodness and faithfulness. And help
me always point to You in praise, remembering that all good
things come from You. In Jesus' name I pray. Amen.

Love, Love, Love

This is how we have discovered love's reality: Jesus sacrificed his life for us. Because of this great love, we should be willing to lay down our lives for one another. If anyone sees a fellow believer in need and has the means to help him, yet shows no pity and closes his heart against him, how is it even possible that God's love lives in him?

1 JOHN 3:16–17 TPT

If you could sum up the Bible in one word, it would be *love*. Everything the Lord has done has been because of love. Think of how He restored Joseph and redeemed Rahab. See how He blessed Abraham and saved the Israelites from Egyptian slavery. And it's because God loves us so deeply that He sent His Son, Jesus, to pay the price for the sin that separated us from our Creator.

It's because of His great love for you that you can pass that love on to others with gusto. You can show care and concern because He did first. You can have compassion for others because of Jesus. And when God sees you passing on the love and care and compassion you've received, He calls your choices beautiful.

. . . .

Father, thank You for giving me the ability to love myself, You, and others. I know it's because of You I can live and love with intentionality. Help my heart stay soft so I can give my best to those around me. In Jesus' name I pray. Amen.

Incompatible

Don't set the affections of your heart on this world or in loving the things of the world. The love of the Father and the love of the world are incompatible. For all that the world can offer us—the gratification of our flesh, the allurement of the things of the world, and the obsession with status and importance—none of these things come from the Father but from the world. This world and its desires are in the process of passing away, but those who love to do the will of God live forever.

1 JOHN 2:15-17 TPT

This powerful passage of scripture is an important warning not to love the things of the world above God. His way is not the world's way. They are not compatible. And the trap is set for us to care too much about the here and now rather than hold on to the promises of eternity.

Sweet one, God desires all your heart because He knows the beauty it holds inside. He knows the plans He's created just for you. And because He's a jealous God, His hope is that you'll crave a relationship with Him over anything the world can offer.

....

Father, I confess there are times the world's offerings are enticing. It's not easy to look past the trendy and popular. I need Your help to keep my eyes fixed on You instead. Make my heart long for You above all. In Jesus' name I pray. Amen.

Beautiful Tears of Authenticity

Then tears streamed down Jesus' face.
JOHN 11:35 TPT

Tears are a powerful expression of emotion. Some people may cry more easily than others, but every one of us needs the cleansing power of a good cry from time to time. Even Jesus cried. Maybe God included this tidbit of information in His Word so we'd understand the importance of it.

Some of us were raised with parents who told us crying was a sign of weakness, so we learned to stuff our emotions. Some of us have been ridiculed because tears are a response to so many emotions, from being tired to being hungry to being excited. Some people use tears as a tool of manipulation or a way to punish or shame others. Crying can be complex.

But can't you imagine the compassion God felt when He saw His Son's tears streaming down His face? That same compassion extends to you too. To God, authentic tears are a beautiful expression of your heart, and He is quick to comfort when you ask. He collects those tears and promises healing and restoration. Go ahead and have a good cry. And invite God into that flood of emotion.

....

*Father, sometimes I am so overwhelmed with sadness and
heartbreak that I can't help but cry out my pain. And so often,
I cry alone. Would You be near me in those moments? I could
use Your comfort and peace. In Jesus' name I pray. Amen.*

It's Not All Up To You

If you don't have all the wisdom needed for this journey, then all you have to do is ask God for it; and God will grant all that you need. He gives lavishly and never scolds you for asking.

JAMES 1:5 VOICE

Don't worry, friend. You don't need to know it all. You don't need to have everything figured out. It's not all up to you. What a relief!

At some point in your life, you decided you had to play god. Rather than trust that He was in control—that He had the answers you needed in your relationships, finances, career, parenting, and personal life—you put yourself in His position. You chose to trust your wisdom above God's wisdom. And chances are, that decision eventually landed you in a mess more than once.

The Lord finds beauty in your willingness to ask for His help. He's pleased when you recognize how much you need His understanding and discernment, and invite Him in. Choosing to seek His advice tells God that you recognize His leadership in your life. And in His great love for you, He promises to bless you for it.

. . . .

Father, I confess I've been conditioned to figure things out on my own. The world tells us we're fully capable of making our own choices. But I'm learning to recognize my human limitations, and I need Your help to know the next right step. In Jesus' name I pray. Amen.

The Beauty of Being Teachable

A fool is in love with his own opinion,
but wisdom means being teachable.
PROVERBS 12:15 TPT

Decide today to be a woman who is teachable instead of someone who thinks their way is the best way. Being open to learning is a beautiful trait that yields beautiful results. And while it's not always easy to accept discipline or constructive criticism, choosing to listen is a wise move. We're not perfect, right?

The truth is that making some small changes (or maybe some big ones!) might be extremely beneficial as we navigate life. Maybe if some of our ways of thinking or acting were tweaked a bit, we would get better results in life. And getting advice from someone who's been there and done that can help us avoid pitfalls we may not even see.

You may be smart and even wise. You may have a history of great choices. You may even be the one others come to for advice. But also be someone who is teachable and moldable. God considers that kind of humility a beautiful trait, and He will bless you for it.

....

Father, I don't want to be right in my own eyes. I don't want to
be stubborn, thinking my way is the only right way. Give me the
confidence in You to be teachable. Help me know what advice
to take and what advice to let go. In Jesus' name I pray. Amen.

Numbered Days

*Help us to remember that our days are numbered, and help
us to interpret our lives correctly. Set your wisdom deeply
in our hearts so that we may accept your correction.*

PSALM 90:12 TPT

When the Lord thought you up, He made sure every detail was covered. From your hair color to your height to your skin tone, God chose. He decided what family you'd be born into and, if not the same, what family would raise you. He knew where you'd live, what your talents would be, what foods you'd like to eat, and everything in between. And most importantly, God knew the exact day you'd enter the world as well as the day you'd see Him face-to-face. Your days are numbered, so it's important to use them wisely.

Be the kind of woman who lives with intentionality. Find out what your passion is, and fight for it. Discover your purpose and walk it out. Don't let pride or stubbornness keep you from making the most of each day. God created a beautiful life for you, and you can honor Him by embracing it with gusto.

....

*Father, I don't want to waste my time living for the wrong things.
Instead, I want to make my life count. I want to walk out the plans
You have for me. And I want others to know You more because
of how I choose to live. In Jesus' name I pray. Amen.*

The Beauty of Holding Back

*You can recognize fools by the way they give full vent
to their rage and let their words fly! But the wise bite
their tongue and hold back all they could say.*

PROVERBS 29:11 TPT

How many times have you lost it on someone—like really let them have it? Chances are it's happened a time or two (or ten) in your lifetime. Anger is a real emotion that's hard to rein in at times. But God is clear on what He thinks about rage. He says that throwing a hissy fit turns a person into a fool. That's pretty clear, isn't it?

In contrast, God says that choosing to bite your tongue and refrain from saying the things you really want to say is wisdom. When you want to unleash your fury on another but keep your mouth shut instead, it's honorable. When you want to act in frustration to make your feelings known but don't, your wisdom is recognized by the Lord. And God calls it beautiful.

....

*Father, there are times I want others to pay for upsetting me. Sometimes
I just want them to know my anger is real and justified. Please help me
remember the value of taming my tongue, knowing it shows maturity
on my part. I don't want to be known as an angry woman. I want to be
known for being mindful and wise. In Jesus' name I pray. Amen.*

Choosing Love

*"However, I say to you, love your enemy, bless the one who curses you,
do something wonderful for the one who hates you, and respond
to the very ones who persecute you by praying for them."*
MATTHEW 5:44 TPT

Today's verse is a lofty one. It's one of those verses we sometimes wish God hadn't included in His Word because it asks so much of us. It commands things of us that feel unfair, unwanted, and undeserved by others. God is telling us to walk out our faith in tangible ways and to act in ways that feel unnatural.

God sees the times you struggle to love your enemy but do so anyway. He sees the times you respond in kindness to those who don't like you. He sees the times you choose to extend grace rather than hold someone's mean-spirited actions against them. And He hears the prayers you pray for those who have hurt you. He sees it all, every bit of effort. Sweet one, know that your decision to choose love over payback is incredibly beautiful to Him.

....

*Father, I'll be honest: this principle of choosing love is a hard one
to walk out because people can be so mean. And so often, what I
really want to do is treat them the same way they've treated me.
But even more, I want to live a life that pleases You. Please give
me the courage to do that. In Jesus' name I pray. Amen.*

Called Higher

*It is easy to love those who love you—even a tax collector can
love those who love him. And it is easy to greet your friends—
even outsiders do that! But you are called to something higher:
"Be perfect, as your Father in heaven is perfect."*
MATTHEW 5:46-48 VOICE

We all know that perfection isn't the goal because we're incapable of achieving perfection on any level. God may be perfect and we may be created in His image, but we are flawed. We mess up on the regular, and our best-laid plans fail. But what God wants from you is a willingness to show up to your life and live with purpose. He wants you to choose love when a situation justifies hate. He wants you to forgive when someone's actions don't feel worthy of forgiveness. God wants you to show the world a different way. Friend, God is calling you higher.

Think of people whom you can love better than you are now. Think of situations where you can respond in a way that shows you're a Jesus-girl. And choose now to live the rest of your life in a way that blesses others and glorifies the Lord. Because that is beautiful.

....

*Father, thank You for calling me higher. The choice to go higher
with You—to love others radically—is hard because it goes against
what my flesh wants, but I know it's exactly what You want for me.
Give me strength and grace. In Jesus' name I pray. Amen.*

The Ministry of Presence

Rejoice with those who rejoice [sharing others' joy],
and weep with those who weep [sharing others' grief].
ROMANS 12:15 AMPC

To thrive in community, we need to be willing to meet others right where they are. Be observant, knowing what your friends need. Find the time to show up and be with them no matter what they're facing. Loving this way is called the "ministry of presence," and it speaks volumes to those you care about.

Few things can make someone feel more loved and seen than the simple act of sharing in their joy or grief. Can you remember a time when a friend walked with you through a hard time? Or when they celebrated a victory with you? It meant the world, didn't it? When they took the time and made the effort to be a part of your circumstance, your heart was warmed. In the same way, your willingness to be selfless in these ways blesses others and reveals your heart to God. And He calls it beautiful.

....

Father, what an honor to be able to share in the joys and heartaches of
Your children. Thank You for creating community and for giving me the
opportunity to be Your hands and feet to those around me. I don't take
that lightly. Please help me see those moments of engagement clearly,
and give me the confidence to step into them. In Jesus' name I pray. Amen.

Perfect Timing

The Lord does not delay and is not tardy or slow about what He promises, according to some people's conception of slowness, but He is long-suffering (extraordinarily patient) toward you, not desiring that any should perish, but that all should turn to repentance.

2 PETER 3:9 AMPC

I think we'd all agree that waiting on God to show up when we need Him the most is one of the hardest things we can do. It takes grit to stay focused on His goodness when it seems like He's not listening. It takes guts to put it all in His hands rather than try to fix it ourselves. And it's hard to give up control and have faith when we're desperate to be rescued.

But the fantastic news is that God's timing is always perfect, and our decision to be patient pleases the Lord. He loves a surrendered heart full of faith—faith that believes God will do what needs to be done. So, friend, where do you need to trust God's timing right now? Let Him see your confidence in His plans. Show Him your beautiful faith.

....

Father, I want to be a woman who fully relies on Your promise to complete Your good work in me. I am choosing to believe that Your timing and plan are perfect. And when I struggle, would You help my unbelief? In Jesus' name I pray. Amen.

Be a Woman of Your Word

*God can't stomach liars; he loves the
company of those who keep their word.*
PROVERBS 12:22 MSG

Today's verse is straightforward. . .and powerful. Chances are you have lied more times than you can count. We all have! We've all flat-out lied to save ourselves from trouble as a child or maybe even today in our jobs. We've lied in an effort not to hurt someone else's feelings—for example, when a friend asks if an outfit is flattering or if a new haircut is the bomb. We've also told little white lies, ones we justify as necessary to keep the peace. Yes, we've all lied.

But did you know that no matter the reason, God cannot stomach lies? Regardless of your motives, lies are repulsive to the Lord. And while there is nothing you can do to make Him love you more or less than He does at this very moment, He delights in a woman who tells the truth and keeps her word. God finds that kind of commitment beautiful.

....

*Father, I confess that I have lied countless times in my life.
Please forgive me for not being honest with others, even when I
thought it was the right thing to do. I want my words and actions
to glorify You, and I'm committed to thinking about the things I
say with more intentionality. In Jesus' name I pray. Amen.*

Treat Others How You Want To Be Treated

Think of the kindness you wish others
would show you; do the same for them.
LUKE 6:31 VOICE

If you could create the perfect friend or husband or parent, what would you include? We're not talking about looks, achievements, or financial assets. We're talking about the ways you'd want them to treat you.

What would be on your list? You'd probably want them to treat you with respect and care. You might want them to have compassion and a desire to understand you and your emotions. Maybe you'd want them to be generous with their time and willing to help you when you need it. And you'd probably want honesty and someone who feels safe. What else?

Sweet one, if these are the things you want in others, then let them be the ways you treat those around you. The Bible says you reap what you sow, so be intentional to sow the right things. This kind of intentional treatment reveals a heart that desires the same. To God, kindness is beautiful because it blesses everyone involved.

....

Father, help me be mindful in the way I treat others. I want to be
known for being kind and generous in the way I live and love. Help
me embrace the concept of reaping and sowing, and let it be a driving
force as I interact with those around me. In Jesus' name I pray. Amen.

He'll Do It Again

But in the day that I'm afraid, I lay all my fears before you and trust in you with all my heart. What harm could a man bring to me? With God on my side I will not be afraid of what comes. The roaring praises of God fill my heart, and I will always triumph as I trust his promises.

PSALM 56:3–4 TPT

This passage of scripture sometimes feels impossible to walk out. It's so hard to lay every fear at the feet of Jesus and trust that He will take care of them all. We've become conditioned to jump into control mode as we try to figure things out on our own. We manipulate others or our situation as we try to fix what's making us afraid. So this idea of giving up control is a big deal.

God finds a surrendered heart beautiful. He delights in watching you gird up your faith and give your fears to Him. And He knows that when you spend your time praising Him and recounting all the ways He has taken care of you in the past, you will gain confidence that He'll do it again.

....

Father, I know You have a perfect track record in my life.
I remember the times You have shown up in epic ways.
Help me have the confidence right now to share my fears with
You and then let them go. In Jesus' name I pray. Amen.

The Recipe for Being Blessed

But blessed is the one who trusts in Me alone; the Eternal will be his confidence. He is like a tree planted by water, sending out its roots beside the stream. It does not fear the heat or even drought. Its leaves stay green and its fruit is dependable, no matter what it faces.

JEREMIAH 17:7–8 VOICE

When you trust God alone, the results are unmatched. It means you don't get freaked out by the doctor's report. It means you don't fear the mounting bills in relation to your dwindling bank account. It means you don't lose sleep over the house that's been on the market longer than you'd hoped or the looming deadline that feels like a freight train headed your way. God says you will find blessings when you trust Him rather than stare at your circumstances.

Friend, where do you need to exercise this kind of trust in your life right now? Where are you bogged down in a scary situation and need a change of plans so you can reclaim your serenity? Where is joy being stolen from you these days? God wants to bless His beautiful daughter with peace and confidence. And the recipe calls for faith.

Father, help me focus my eyes and heart on You when my life feels out of control. Give me the ability to trust that You will take care of me through the hard times. I need Your strength and wisdom every day. In Jesus' name I pray. Amen.

A Beautiful Exchange

*So here's what I've learned through it all: Leave all
your cares and anxieties at the feet of the Lord,
and measureless grace will strengthen you.*

Psalm 55:22 TPT

What are your stressors these days? Is your marriage in a tough season? Is parenting harder than you thought, and it feels way above your pay grade? Are friendships feeling unstable? Have you been rejected or abandoned? Are you trying to navigate an epic betrayal? Maybe your parents are showing signs of aging or your credit card bill is out of control. Is your job overwhelming and your future there feels shaky?

So many things can steal your peace and leave you with a mound of worry and anxiety. As long as you're breathing on planet Earth, rest assured you'll struggle with worry on the regular. But God invites you to lay your cares and concerns at His feet and exchange them for His grace. Choosing to make good on His offer delights His heart; this beautiful exchange is a win-win!

....

*Father, the truth is that I'm drowning in fear and worry. I'm scared
of so many things right now. Would You please take them off
my shoulders and replace them with the peace of Jesus? I know
You can make my burdens disappear, and I am asking that of You
today. Please exchange my uncertainty and weakness for Your
grace and strength. I need Your help. In Jesus' name I pray. Amen.*

Your Beautifully Broken Heart

*The LORD is good, a strength and stronghold in the
day of trouble; He knows [He recognizes, cares for,
and understands fully] those who take refuge and trust in Him.*

NAHUM 1:7 AMP

We're all going to face troubles. It may be a marriage marked by tension and you're afraid your spouse is going to walk away. It could be a friend who betrayed you by sharing a sensitive secret that exposed you. Maybe your finances are in trouble because of some unexpected or unavoidable expenses. Maybe you're about to start a treatment plan for an illness or are struggling to find the right medication combination for a condition. It may be that you just feel alone and unloved or are grieving the loss of someone dear to you. Troubles are inevitable.

Don't forget you have a Father standing by with open arms, and He promises to be the strength you need and a stronghold to protect you. So take your beautifully broken heart to the Lord and let Him be your refuge. Choose to put your trust in Him. He is ready and waiting.

....

*Father, my heart is heavy right now with so many fears and worries.
I am scared and angry and sad all at the same time and can't do this
alone. Please grab me up in Your loving arms and comfort me. Help
me rest knowing You will handle it all. In Jesus' name I pray. Amen.*

Scripture Index

OLD TESTAMENT

More Inspiration for Your Beautiful Soul

978-1-64352-637-9

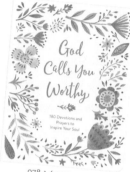

978-1-64352-474-0

These delightful devotionals—created just for you—will encourage and inspire your soul with deeply rooted truths from God's Word. Each devotional reading will assure you that God's Word is unchanging and will help you to grow in your faith as you become the beautifully courageous woman the heavenly Creator intended you to be!

Flexible Casebound / $12.99 each